BRITISH SOCIAL

HISTORY

(1950-2010)

BRITISH SOCIAL HISTORY

(1950-2010)

By Ken Ross

For my children's children

BOOKS BY THIS AUTHOR:

Brainbox, Tables Are Fun, Spooky Towers, The Spy With The Missing Brain, Joke File, Animal Crackers, Yucky Chuckles, School Screamers, Monster Giggles , Fantasy Football, On Your Marks, Master Class: Play Acting, St. Dodgers' School Yearbook, Halloween, Pirate, Code Busters, Dracula, Alien, Werewolf, Frankenstein, Witch, Top Secret, Spy File, Essential School Fun File, Private Detective, Skeleton, Looking For Twiggy, In The Words Of…, What's In Your Memory? British Social History 1950-2010, Dear Dr. Cornflake, More Dear Dr. Cornflake, Nanny Noo & the Ravenous Cannibals, Nanny Noo & The Ravenous Scrapmen, The Lads Will Have Blood, A Cross of Crocuses, Ann: irresistible spirit, An Old Affair, Antiques – Easy Money, Wasted Pain, Protection, Bodies, Mama, Broken Sisters, Goodbye Violet, Rosalee's Punishment, A View of British Politics, Louann's Home Movie, The Last Days of Childhood, Wrapped in Green Comfort, Superfluous, Partial Absolution, happiness Regained, Lizzie, Moira's Sacrifice.

BRITISH SOCIAL HISTORY 1950-2010

Stepping Through Decades

The hum of the tracks on the mainline alerted practiced train spotters to an imminent arrival. Two or three miles distant the streak was approaching, two or three minutes of unrelieved anticipation before the arced line that disappeared near the Leeman Roads sheds would throw forth a train and its coaches to the view of waiting passengers and onlookers on platform 8: not just an engine but a famous locomotive powering its trail from Edinburgh Waverley to London's King's Cross with its accompanying rhythmical tune of tu-tu tu-tu for over four hundred miles.

I and my brother hurried over the bridge, clasping our penny platform tickets, holding our sharpened pencils and dog-eared notebooks, and tucking our elbows to our coats to protect the eggs sandwiches that were to last all the hours of a train spotting day. The woman's voice over the tannoy (her whose nose surely was pinched with a clothes peg) announced, 'The train arriving on platform eight south will form the 10.57 to King's Cross, stopping at...' We sprinted along dodging passengers in chaotic horizontal lines that hugged the platform's edge. Men and women in dull-colored clothing, carrying bags, holding cases and children's hands, wearing expressions of travelers on faces that neither gleamed nor radiated thought.

The hum altered to a drone then became the distinctive sound of an engine approaching and we scanned north to witness the Brunswick green body of an A4 class preceding its Pullman coaches. Avid spotters drew breath, passengers shifted their positions and the aroma of the steam engine absorbed York station's air as Sir Nigel Gresley arrived at a halt before its audience. Doors of the carriages swung onto the lip of the platform, legs flailed as they searched for lower levels of ground, passengers appeared and walked like those who have been seated too long as the spotters rushed to the beautiful spectacle that was listed as 60007 in the annual combine. Like all who pay homage, the men and boys with their biros devoured the blissful sight of the fastest post-war steam engine in the world. Oh yes, Mallard broke the world speed record in 1938 at 126 mph but dear old Sir Nigel achieved 110 mph in 1959 with a full complement of passengers in its carriages.

Within minutes Sir Nigel Gresley had departed on its journey south and soon my brother and I were on platform 9 talking to Mrs. Rousterby the ice-cream lady who lived in the terrace houses near Holgate Bridge. She spoiled us with lollies; my brother visited her long after we were very young children, and in an age when the diesel had taken over from the steam locomotive. This scene from the early Sixties remains clear long after others have faded: a first taste of being unaccompanied for many hours in the bowels of a moving society where industry was never still, and people were continually coming and going. As a child of eight years the fascination with the sounds, smells, and frequent bursts of energy that gave life to York's railway station promoted thoughts of social inquiry as to how communal life evolved and how in my future, I should evolve with it. It occurred to me then that a train driver's daily routine differed from the station porter's and how my time scurrying from one platform to another was much less interesting than the time of the passenger who had journeyed from Edinburgh to London.

Only a decade later and social deprivation greeted a couple of newlyweds to adulthood. Young love blossoms through all ages and it must bear the consequences of its desires. She and I found our first home in a single room with the first week's rent of three pounds borrowed from my maternal grandmother. Situated in a Victorian terrace at cosmopolitan Potternewton in Leeds' inner-city this thoroughly despicable bedsit offered nothing in the shape of comfort or luxury. We had viewed it briefly, too briefly to satisfy our sanity, picked up the keys, and entered the place of our own volition. Our newfound sense of liberation and smiles quickly evaporated in the dismal 30 square feet that was now home.

We opened our bags to expose a few meager possessions and as independent people decided to put the kettle on to prepare water for a cup of tea. We owned tea bags, a pair of cups but a shilling was required for the gas meter – such are the hardships discovered by young adventurers who have relied on their parents for 18 years. Then life delivered a shocking reality, the crooked landlord had rigged his meters for before the water had boiled the gas ran out: already expenditure had reached £3 1s and my weekly wage amounted to just £9.

There was no need to discuss the financial stress of the immediate future or to consider putting a second shilling in the meter. My work was over twenty miles away in Keighley, train fares and bus fares were essential if only to retain the prospect of further wages. We sat on the bed, snuggled together like beggars in a cold doorway, and allowed our minds to settle on the predicament we had willingly encountered.

Minutes later it worsened. The damp from the mattress seeped into our clothing – we were sitting on a huge smelly sponge that likely housed creatures more commonly found in lagoons. We did not laugh, we didn't despair, and we got off the bed and faced it with wonderment in our eyes. And our eyes ventured upwards to the wall where soaking mossy green wallpaper was breeding bacteria in a multitude of farms.

'I'll go to the council,' she said, 'apply for a flat. We might get one in a few months.' We went for a walk to see our friends in Harehills, probably refreshed in spirit to have temporarily left a huge mistake behind. The resilience of youth pumped faster as our steps guided us back to dreams of what may be in our future and by the time we had told our friends of a place of our own it had become not so daunting, not as horrific as the shock had told us.

However, economies had to be ever-present in our thoughts and we deprived ourselves of a bag of chips each and bought six 4d 7oz tins of Heinz beans which we hoped would last us until payday. Later that day we spent our last coins on six eggs from a Polish shop in Potternewton only to find that they had purple yokes. I had no doubt this was social history in the making: this was a tale of ordinary people setting out in life and it bore the stains of reality. Historians could embellish reality, exaggerate its influences, or make it appear a singular reality. Though young and inexperienced it was becoming clear that realities are as numerous as those who perceive them.

Ten years later as an early evening September sun warmed the garden and the whole village of Fairburn in North Yorkshire a kinder society was in our midst. The fresh air, open fields, country colors, and earth's wild creatures complimented a peaceful existence that city life was never so generous to afford. We stepped into the garden, four children, a baby playing in her pram, with hands filled with containers to hold the fruits we were about to harvest. On next door's drive Graham and his son Shane were repairing a motorcycle, 'More blackberries?' he said.

The kids ran about on the long decline that fell to a small valley below the garden's end. Charlie, our other neighbor, was preparing his load for a bird-watching trip to Europe; his meek tiny wife looked on like a maid who dared not speak to her master. Their two children stood motionless probably wondering why their father was leaving them once more. 'The sun is shining,' I said laconically. 'It is,' replied Charlie.

Blackberry bushes skirted the full perimeter of the rear garden and each day through the weeks of September we plucked them of their ripened fruit. It was a precarious job that left the arms and hands covered in scratches for the blackberry bush appears to have a mind of its own and lashes out its deadly strands at will. Our containers filled quickly as we moved down the garden, the children would keep eating them until their mother warned of bellyache if they ate too many. Later we made blackberry pies and placed pounds of them in plastic bags in the freezer for my aunty and my father who both turned them into jam.

Blackberry picking for us could last more than an hour and proved an annual delight that few city dwellers experience. After, we'd sit on the grass, pour a glass of pop for the kids, and listening to the day's closing bird songs. This too was social history in the making. I used to think then that a similar scene could have occurred one or two centuries before, that all that had changed were the clothes we wore and the containers in which the blackberries were collected, but social habits have an innate right to continue if they are pleasurable and unifying. For only a brief period of my adult life, the countryside was home and as with my childhood's small-town upbringing, it helped shape a fuller view of people in their homesteads.

Another ten years and Thatcher's social revolution was nearing its ending with so many having risen in status and so many had suffered from the great correction that Britain desperately needed before she came to power. This ten-year period brought changes aplenty for the boy who watched passengers board Sir Nigel Gresley's carriages and depart south to places unknown.

Standing before 250 children in the school dinner hall wearing a shirt and tie and looking every inch the teacher in control I said firmly, 'Hands together... Let us say grace.' A congregation of friends whose names became as familiar as their personalities clasped their small hands and began, 'for what we are about to receive...' It is a privilege to guide young lives and to be entrusted by the school's headmistress to play a key role in daily routines is indeed not simply a job but a special honor.

As the children commenced dinner, I began my usual parade around the tables, ensuring each child was comfortable and eating, correcting bad behavior, and pausing for brief chats to answer the many questions which young ones ask. From assisting in the nursery to keeping accounts and being the watchful eye that governed safety in the school my life had become a necessary and somewhat hectic three-way servitude to children.

In the playground, a boy yelled 'Miss! Please, Miss!' Turning to find a joyful face and a hand thrusting out a chocolate bar he added, 'I've brought you a present.' Such kindnesses and acts of thoughtfulness by children to those they see as their mentors in school are beautiful displays of innocence. Robert Duncan will be remembered in my mind as I shall be in his.

When duties were done, I rushed home to work for a few hours on my second occupation relating to children. Commissions were coming regularly for my educational and humorous books for youngsters and at this moment in my life, there was no shortage of children to inspire my writing. It was a rather odd circumstance when books were published for teachers at the school who requested signed copies, making me feel like an unwilling celebrity rather than the easy-going bloke who wandered up and down the corridors ensuring things were running smoothly.

A few more pages crafted or drafted then down the hill and back to school to pick up my youngest four before the eldest four returned home from work and other schools. Time had changed the complexion of fortune in so many ways: now a single parent almost every minute of each day was devoted to work in one form or another. I looked on the hardship philosophically realizing that in a dozen or so years (approximately) I'd be as free as a bird. Every cloud has a sprinkling of gold dust! The benefits of being involved in such a large social circle, from being a 'mother' in the schoolyard to playing the role of the Headmistress's sidekick to a daily supermarket shopper and the local bloke who writes books, were comfort indeed for a father of eight who might have appeared somewhat unlucky in life.

The century turned and brought with it radical changes to a previously local existence. I'd learned to drive, bought a car, and had arrived at Butlins' Holiday Camp with my two youngest and we were about to experience our first vacation, if only for a weekend. The occasion celebrated my parents' fiftieth wedding anniversary and all my siblings and their families were there too. This perhaps did not equal Scott's expedition to the Antarctic in other people's eyes but from my perspective, it seemed an extraordinary giant step.

Standing by the go-kart race track watching my son out-battle his uncles on the turns brought a smile to a face that had lately become too serious. My motive to create had withered in the late Nineties and mundane simple pleasures seemed my recipe for amusement. Watching people enjoy themselves refreshes the spirits but appears an interest without a purpose. My daughter beside me was getting excited by her brother's antics and I wondered how it would feel when these two children were both speeding away and I was left mulling over memories of them being little as all parents do with time.

The interaction between aunties, uncles, cousins, children, grandchildren, parents, nephews and nieces and grandparents came all so easy for everyone as they played on a slot machine, watched shows, shopped, ate ice-creams and partook of everything that was on offer; they were social creatures exploring the pleasures of relationships and being perfectly natural in these surroundings. From all parts of the country they had traveled here, not a usual holiday for some, but nevertheless, a coming together of family members strung across a range of social classes to celebrate a triumph of marriage.

A dinner party ensued with a huge cake being presented to my parents. There were toasts and expressions of love and congratulations. This new holiday feeling was different: I didn't know what to make of it but it certainly entranced the children. As the party rang out in merriment I was occupied with the question of whether witnessing a social event was the same as being a part of the event. Surely a greater degree of objectivity is required from the witness than from the participant?

By 2010 the age of the internet and mass communication prevailed and many old social habits fell by the wayside; the mobile phone and the computer became kings of social interaction. On the home scene, my youngest daughter was now married with two young boys and they all lived with me, what is more, we were all computer addicts with our own machines. A home confined by walls which to all previous generations had meant closure to interaction with the outside world was no longer true. Furthermore, my life beyond the home reached new territories.

I'd taken a part-time job as a home shopping delivery driver and found myself visiting places whose names had been familiar for years. Delivering shopping to hundreds of cities, suburbs, towns, villages, farms, and remote houses gave me fresh insight into how and where people lived. This opportunity to meet thousands of individuals on their doorsteps revealed information on their living habits which I previously could only have estimated from a much smaller sample.

Seeing into homes revealed changes in décor, in furniture, in sparseness and clutter, in cleanliness and security, in wealth or poverty, and into the interests of occupiers. Eating habits were revealed in the types of foods I delivered and both manners and the nuances of communication between family members were on show.

The population had so obviously expanded during my lifetime and the multiculturalism of modern-day Britain could be glimpsed at first hand from a journey in any town or city. Even road systems, navigation, scenery, amenities, the unspoiled spaces of this green and pleasant land became visible on my rounds through the varied landscapes of Northern England. A few days each week I lived the life of those I had seen board Sir Nigel Gresley's coaches in the distant past. The small boy who had so wondered what the life of the engine driver or a passenger may be like was traversing the highway and byways finding pockets of interest in each passing hour. Few pursuits in my life have been so educational in terms of understanding the nature of people in society than glimpsing them in their places of residence where they are generally at ease and without pretension.

I discovered rare beauty in ideal settings, found families cramped in single rooms, witnessed both dirt and disinfectant in the space of minutes, politeness and ignorance in the same home, helplessness, and helpfulness side by side on the same street, thieves, and protectors in the same neighborhoods, attitudes of gratitude and miserly moaners, those who embraced modernity and those who shunned its shine.

The nature of people has likely changed little from age to age but the behavior of people is in some way influenced by how social change affects their daily lives. The endless need to progress and the evidence of personal progress are apparent in the homes of the British and the symbols of this desire can be seen everywhere.

If I wish to progress with meaning on my path I need to return to the hum of the mainline track and be alerted to that practiced trainspotters know is coming: two or three months distant a book is approaching, two or three months of unrelieved anticipation before the final full stop brings it to a halt and then I can listen again and keep on listening for the remainder of my life.

Collecting Evidence

On whose evidence is history founded? Peel away the layers of the mind and take it back to the very earliest memories of history that arrive by way of teaching or reading experiences or by visiting places. The early memories do not crumble; they are starting points for journeys of discovery and for adventures in former times to minds that will never settle or be satisfied with stagnation. We absorb rudimentary facts that form the foundation stones of our learning and on which we build the interests of a future that hopefully will be both enlightening and rewarding. These initial tastes of education are taken on trust and it is not until we question them and sort out their significance and validity that we begin to make better judgments on information that comes our way. History sometimes deludes us, influences our thinking, colors our prejudices, and exalts some to positions higher than their achievements deserve. It has the capacity to overstate, the brushes to tarnish and the selective memory to forget that which is worthy of remembrance.

We can with one eye closed looked upon British History as the story of Kings and Queens, of Generals and War Leaders, of Churches and Religious Leaders, of Poets and Artists, of Politicians and Practitioners and we shall read differing accounts of the people we were and the lofty heights we climbed to as a race of people. The rudimentary facts of history such as Henry VIII had six wives of whom two were executed, that the Duke of Wellington defeated Napoleon at Waterloo, that Thomas Becket was murdered by knights at Canterbury in 1170, that Shelley, Keats, and Wordsworth were great romantic poets, or that Churchill became Prime Minister again at 76 tell us only a minute fraction of the story that is to tell of British History. For every person that has ever lived in this kingdom a history has perished or has been recorded. History should not choose its content and disregard the content of its minor contributors: significance only highlights itself against a background of ordinariness but that which is ordinary plays a major role in any balanced view of the past.

Present-day archaeologists are unearthing remnants related to the social history of past times. Fascinating discoveries paint pictures of lives that were forgotten because once they were unworthy of preservation or documentation. Our preconception with the notable and the great had hitherto focussed primarily on what was big and exceptional and that which lead society rather than that which formed the mass of society. But there can be as much wealth in owning coins as there can be in owning notes and tiny historical details will always illuminate our understanding of any age.

The bulk of my reading of British History has dealt with events, innovation, wars, literary and artistic figures, royalty and nobility, architecture and culture, politics and science, philosophy and theory, discovery and adventure, conquest, and religion. So interesting and enthralling was each footstep that found a course from one century to another, going backward and forwards, sideways and on geographical paths, that there was no inkling to pause to wonder what had been omitted. There is no relenting in the search to complete the whole picture, and never a place to rest for pathways open up with each new revelation. The delightful journey through history is like entering a maze with each successive entrance showing off a hundred more entrances. An adventurer can walk for years only occasionally feeling he has trodden a spot before but never feeling that he has trodden all spots.

About thirty years ago I stumbled upon G. M. Trevelyan's English Social History, first published 1942, and wandering through the magnificent chapters I quickly realized that a man was telling a tale of an extraordinary England that spanned six hundred years. The insight he gives into the lives of common people is remarkable and he creates the impression that each of us contributes to social history in our peculiar way. We see life how it really unfolded and read about what common folk did and what their societies were like. Trevelyan crafted a new and refreshing approach to looking at the past and gave his readers a perspective that other historians chose to ignore or hadn't found so beguiling or interesting.

The social history of people of any age has bundles to offer, and it should never be left unrecorded. Each aspect of life, from the beds we sleep in, to the coffins in which we are disposed of, reveals something about the way we are. There is nothing uninteresting about existence; no single item or a single habit should be buried by time. What we own tells others who we are and what we do defines what kind of people we become. We understand the importance of progress after we recognize it has occurred. We are astounded in so many ways by the multifarious threads of history and by what each thread offers in the way of learning about mankind's development.

Year upon year of reading history creates a history of its own. From those early memories of learning have sprung thousands of branches that collectively give us a greater insight into the worlds of our forefathers and from any period in our sphere of learning we can derive particular appreciation of a single happening or of something that stirs us. The history of man is a rich collection of recorded data and in many ways mirrors our own life: in the beginning, man was primitive and knew little, and as children, we were in much the same state. Both history and individuals prosper with progress and what is worth leaving behind shall be left as legacies to coming generations. Just as the archaeologists are currently adding to the legacy with findings of forgotten detail in this book I seek to record the details that an age of rapid change may find fit to neglect.

A lifetime covering the sixty years from 1950 to 2010 witnessed more sociological changes than in any age in the history of man. This record is a personal collection of things that I have noted, and it is my recollections of them rather than the encyclopedia-type description of these things that I leave. A personal experience tells one man's story, and it is always a different story than that told by another individual or by a narrative based on consensus.

Almost everything has changed in the period covered by this book; there follows 200 assorted observations on this time, but many others have remained notes which are worthy of mentioning. The opening scene at York Railways Station has been tossed into modernity with cleaner fresher platforms and diesel trains boarded by passengers in designer named clothing. Sixty years ago, there were still more people yet to be hanged in these islands for capital punishment crimes and the idea of central heating in all homes proved still only a vision of the future.

In the Sixties children's medicals took place in schools, spectacles were somewhat plain and unattractive, contraception wasn't as freely available and as varied as it is today, and Death Duties were causing landowners to give up their grand homes because they had no hope of paying crippling taxes. The towns and cities were lit by smaller, dimmer streetlamps constructed from iron or concrete which could be viewed through the thousands of rattling sash windows that still filled spaces in many cold houses' walls. On city streets litter danced the fandango to the tune of the wind and people were kept warm with pancakes and stew with dumplings.

There were no computers in my childhood for a technological age was unimaginable and a day at the seaside seemed one of the wonders of life. Even foreign holidays were generally the preserve of those who 'had a few quid' and so too was the luxury of possessing the means to run both hot and cold water.

The third quarter of the Twentieth Century still had mums and dads with specific tasks in the home, old men carried pocket watches in their waistcoats and women had curlers in their hair. Marriage was popular, so too chips and mashed potato, shoes had laces and lighter fuel refilled lighters made of stainless steel. The kids were protected by metal fireguards and fenders when they wore their pajamas which were held up with chords.

What a quaint world with crisps and peanuts on pub bars and a majority of workers never having to work shifts. The voting age was 21 and weights were pounds and ounces. Even keeping pigs and chickens persisted in rural areas, there was no texting but there were millions of glass bottles. Directions were not a sat-nav but a signpost hidden in the hedgerow or guidance from a man wearing Brylcreem not hair gel.

Did boys really wear school caps? Yes, they did. Mother wore a whalebone corset, probably a flowered dress, and certainly tights or stockings. In the Fifties and Sixties, a majority of working-class people had never been to an airport, they hadn't heard the words cultural-mix and likely harbored some racial attitudes that were very unpleasant by today's standards.

Furniture was hard and uncomfortable, fish and chips shops were fruitful businesses, paperboys patrolled their rounds, and town centers boasted hoards of shoppers because the suburban shopping centers simply didn't exist. And music... that is a history in itself.

The attitudes and expectations of post-war Britons changed dramatically to the more sophisticated and broader aspirations of today's generations. Some things that history discards are for the benefit of all people and other things provoke sentimentality for ages that will never return.

A LOOK BACK THROUGH TIME

1. The whistling kettle proved a popular method of boiling water after people changed from cooking on a fire to using a cooker. A tin kettle on a gas ring quickly heated water. For the first time, housewives were warned of water boiling as the whistle resounded throughout the house. A high pitch sound resulted from compressed steam being pushed through a narrow kettle spout. Some kettles had a whistle cap fitted to the kettle's spout.

2. Spangles were a sweet with a wonderful name: they became a favorite of many children in the Fifties and the Sixties. They were round-edge flat square shape sweets with a hollow in each side; several flavors came in each packet, and at one time each sweet was individually wrapped.

3. Going to the pictures, or cinema, secured a weekly treat for millions of ordinary folks. Film stars became the idols of the masses; their looks and habits were copied and created fashions and trends. Entrance to the pictures was inexpensive and many picture houses showed lots of films in all areas of town. From the usherette who patrolled the aisles in the interval between films, customers were able to purchase ice-creams, popcorn, and drinks. Going to the pictures was amongst the most common dates for boys and girls.

4. Candles were a necessity in every household. Many places, even within the house, were in darkness, and electric power supplies were not so reliable or as efficient as they later

became. Various shops sold candles, and they were regularly bought by the dozen or half dozen rather than singly.

5. Lots of girls sported the pigtail hairstyle. Often each pigtail was plaited and decorated with a ribbon. The style was tidy and made it less likely the hair would get infected with nits which were rife in some schools.

6. Trams and trolleybuses transported people inside large cities. Trams ran on rails embedded in the roads and trolleybuses depended on overhead powered lines which obstructed the views from the streets. Both vehicle types had designated routes and carried hundreds of thousands of passengers daily. Each had a driver, and also a conductor whose job it was to collect fares.

7. Until the popularisation of television in the late Fifties radio was the major source of home entertainment. Radio programs were commonly known and favorite ones had millions of followers. Radio provided the most instant news source, and it was the medium on which people heard songs for the first time. People sat around the radio to hear major announcements and whole families eagerly listened to broadcast plays and comedy shows. Weather updates and news broadcasts also gained popular followings.

8. Outside toilets persisted well into the Sixties and many terraced streets had special toilet blocks where the urinals were situated. For those with a garden the toilet was usually located in a shed: they were very cold in winter and cisterns were prone to freeze.

9. Before decimalization in the very early Seventies, the coinage structure in England included a five-pound note, a one-pound

note, a ten-shilling note, half a crown, two-shilling piece, one shilling piece, sixpenny bit, threepenny bit, penny, halfpenny, and before 1961 the farthing. Pennies were large and heavy and there were 240 to the pound.

10. The general custom of society was for a man to wear a hat. Cloth caps and trilbies were popular. A man would politely doff his hat when greeting someone he knew, especially if it was a lady. Hat wearing started declining in the Fifties and by the late Sixties became a custom more associated with the elderly.

11. Brewing tea leaves in a teapot prevailed for decades as the most popular method of making a drink. The British loved tea and its appeal straddled all social classes. By adding boiling water to a large teapot, four cups of tea or more could be served. Tea was purchased in small quarter-pound bags, with larger bags also available. Fortune tellers used to read the tea leaves in the bottom of a cup and from their formation claim to interpret the drinker's fate or fortune. The loose tea leaf fell from favor especially during the Seventies; tea bags though invented much earlier grew in popularity and were more convenient to use. As a consequence of teabags replacing loose leaves, teapots too declined in use as bags could be set individually in cups.

12. Houses with decent size gardens were too pricey for the working classes and the allotment remained a place to grow vegetables for the family. For a small annual cost, men from the terraces were able to feel like landowners with their small plots on which valuable fresh food could be managed.

Flowers too were cultivated, and some people kept chickens for the eggs they produced.

13. Leather footballs had an inner bladder which after insertion was inflated to a suitable pressure. The opening for the bladder was laced. Dubbin was used to waterproof the outer core of the ball, however, when wet conditions prevailed footballs became very heavy and it proved exceedingly difficult to kick them far. Heading a wet football was a dicey affair and certainly pained the neck muscles.

14. The Spirograph achieved popularity as a toy of the Sixties. With round plastic discs that contained holes for the pen point, a child was able to produce perfect arced and circular designs that were unlike anything created by hand. A variety of pieces came with each set. Each piece was edged with teeth that rolled along the teeth of other pieces.

15. Seafood stalls attracted lots of customers at seaside resorts. Long stretches of the ground by harbors were occupied by stallholders selling wares that carried a unique odor of sea life. Black whelk shells littered the sidewalks, so too the remains of consumed crabs. Seaside visitors brought these wares back to the city as treats for themselves and friends.

16. Almost every parade of shops contained a butcher's shop. Each butcher gave personal service and knew the likes of his customers, including whether or not to offer a dog bone for the family pet. Most pre-1970s housewives bought their Sunday roast from a local butcher.

17. Secondary schools, predominantly, consisted of same-sex pupils. The thought of boys and girls mixing for education purposes was generally deemed too distracting for

adolescents. At dinnertimes, girls' schools frequently had a small crowd of boys at the railings, and one or two girls may be bold enough to lurk outside a boys' secondary school too.

18. Every cellar or kitchen in a house was fitted with a fuse box. It was essential that at least the male of the household could change a fuse, for they often blew and left the rooms in complete darkness. Most people kept a small supply of different strength fuses, and neighbors were often called upon to lend a fuse if the correct one was not available at the time of a fuse blowing.

19. Many drinks in glass bottles cost more to those who didn't take their bottles back to the shop. A refundable deposit of around 3d was paid on a bottle. When times were hard families collected their bottles and returned them to the shop. Frequently a few shillings retrieved could see a family through another day or two.

20. The small pool of Christian names could not compare with the vast assortment of those today. An unusual name was rare indeed. Every class of children in days gone by would contain at least one David, Stephen, John, or Christopher and certainly a girl named Anne, Mary, Margaret, or Elizabeth. Registrars were much stricter with the names given to children and in some places, permission to register a child with an unusual name would be refused.

21. Rag and bone carts pulled by a single horse regularly toured the streets. In exchange for scrap or rags some ragmen would offer balloons or goldfish, others a few coins, and others nothing at all. As they wandered the streets the cry of 'Any old iron, rag bone' could be heard loud and clear.

22. A majority of homes would have at least one Bible. The Bible was the most popular book in the world and modern printing methods brought about its mass production in small volumes. Large family tome versions died out. The giving of a Bible as a gift, especially to a child, prevailed well into the Fifties.

23. The words please and thank you were more widely used. It was regarded as bad manners for a request not to be followed by a please and likewise to not be thanked for service was deemed somewhat ignorant. Manners were instilled into most children and this resulted in a largely polite society.

24. The popular washing powder Omo was known by everyone. Its regular advertisements on the television made it the most famous of brands and the familiar red, white, and blue box could be found in millions of households.

25. Pipe smoking was usually a habit of older men. Though not as widespread as cigarette smoking it had life-long adherents but was found unappealing by the youth of the Sixties. Some who had pipe smoked all their lives had flattened teeth where the pipe sat in their mouths.

26. Single glazed windows were fitted in almost every British house in the Fifties and Sixties. Although double glazing began in the United States as long ago as the Thirties it was unaffordable for the average man in Britain. Not until around 1980 were people having other ideas about their windows, and from this time single-glazing declined steadily.

27. The vest was an essential item of clothing for men and boys. A vest was usually worn under the shirt, and a man may strip

down to his vest in the summer, or to do gardening or to perform physical work. Many men shaved or washed wearing only a vest above the waist. The popularity of the vest diminished greatly in the Sixties as T-shirts found favor.

28. Left-handedness was thought to be a curse of the Devil as late as the Fifties. Indeed, all kinds of measures were taken to prevent left-handedness, some quite barbaric by today's standards. In schools, lefties were punished. Some parents dreaded 'the curse' being manifest in their children. A majority eventually conformed to right-handedness but time has shown that it is perfectly natural to be left-handed.

29. Shoes were expensive and people used cobblers regularly for repairs. Soling and heeling ensured a pair of worn shoes continued to be useful. Many handymen had a last among their tools and often soled and heeled shoes to save money.

30. The simple game of snakes & ladders amused families for hours. The shaking of dice determined how many squares to move on the board. If a player landed at the bottom of a ladder he ascended the board. And if a player landed on the head of a snake he fell to the square at the tail of the snake.

31. Heavy metal typewriters with inked ribbons were once the state of the art writing accessory. They became lighter and more portable when the machines were made of plastic and housed in cases. However, the new typewriters had a brief life of a couple of decades because computers came along and included word processors which did the job of page setting more efficiently.

32. Thousands of stray dogs roamed the streets of Britain and the mongrel outnumbered all other breeds. As late as the

Seventies it was unsurprising to see several dogs in a pack on an estate. A change in social attitudes to the acceptability of stray dogs, together with biting incidents and increased road traffic, greatly reduced the number of wandering dogs by the end of the Twentieth Century.

33. The wooden front garden gate was the entrance point to properties with land. A simple path usually led directly to the front door. These gates had a catch for closing and it was common for whole streets to sport identically designed gates at each garden entrance.

34. Racially offensive words were used frequently until the Seventies when slowly they began to become socially unacceptable. They had persisted even on television programs in the Sixties. As societies grew increasingly multicultural the use of these vulgar words declined, and in later times the most offensive words were outlawed.

35. Eider feathered pillows comforted the head when sleeping. Those who used them will remember the feather ends which occasionally poked through the cloth and scratched the skin. These pillows lasted many years but were gradually replaced by foam ones from the Sixties onward.

36. Swearing came much less frequently to people's lips in the third quarter of the Twentieth Century. People did swear occasionally, but it was more in anger, or during accidents. Many parents wouldn't dream of cursing in front of their children. Indeed, in workplaces, it was frowned upon to swear, and in some places, it would be a cause of dismissal. As the century unfolded swearing became increasingly more socially acceptable.

37. Perhaps the closest a working-class person came to foreign food was eating spaghetti. The English diet was of vegetables and meat, potatoes, and dairy products. Chinese takeaways were early indications that the British were expanding their taste and in the Sixties, there were a few on high streets. But foreign foods took off in a big way and by the end of the century supermarkets offered choices for the taste buds that were once unimaginable.

38. One of the primary social changes has been the playing habits of children. Throughout the first half of the Twentieth Century, the streets and the playgrounds were the main areas occupied by children at play. In the following years, most people could look from their windows and see children at play in the near vicinity with groups of boys playing football and girls juggling balls or playing hopscotch. The outside world was not thought to be a dangerous place for children, indeed, very early in their lives, children were permitted to roam a certain distance from home by their parents. Three major factors altered what had been a normal practice for families. A series of child murders by strangers caused parents to be more cautious and to be a trifle more discriminating of where their children were allowed to go unaccompanied. The second determining factor was the rapid proliferation of motor vehicles: roads were transformed from silent, safe places into hazardous highways where children were in peril. Scarcely a street survived as a play area, and for children to be restricted to the garden necessitated a restriction of those who were welcomed to play. Hence what previously had been a

collected community of children became separate lots of one or two friends. And as the century ended children were enticed to the inner house by the hugely entertaining computers and games consoles. The streets that were once overflowing were now empty.

39. Heavy metal dustbins with large circular metal lids were rubbish deposit points. Each household had a dustbin, usually in the back garden or in terraced streets in an allocated yard. These bins over time became very smelly, especially if rainwater had entered the body of the bin and mixed with waste at the bottom. The dustbin man would have to lift these burdens to his shoulder, carry them to the wagon, empty them, and return them to where he had found them. The metal dustbin survived to the Nineties but its departure was widely welcomed.

40. The tin bath just about made it to the Sixties, but they were becoming rare. In former times this large object was kept in an outhouse or hung on a nail on an outside wall. On bath night it was brought to the front of the fire and filled with pans of hot water. The children often bathed first and then were put to bed. Fresh hot water was added to the bath so that parents may bathe in privacy. Then the very pans which filled the bath emptied it, and bath night was complete for another week.

41. It was something of a special treat for a woman to go to the hairdressers, or to have the hairdresser visit her home. To prolong the effectiveness of the hairdo women wore hairnets, which they removed at the weekend when they wished to look their best.

42. It is probably true to say that many people of the post-war years knew as many hymns as they did songs. The popular church hymns such as 'All Things Bright And Beautiful' were known by all. Hymnbooks sold very well. Hymns were sung daily in schools and filled the morning hours of Sunday radio.

43. The notion that marriage was for life took a severe battering from the late Fifties. The divorce rate rocketed by five hundred percent in about thirty-five years. By the mid-Nineties, many began to question whether marriage would survive as an institution. Where it was once unthinkable for people to live together those who proverbially 'lived in sin' almost equaled in number those who chose marriage.

44. Goldfish in round glass bowls were a common feature in living rooms. In many cases, they had been won at fairgrounds and became a child's first taste of responsibility towards another living creature.

45. The idea of purchasing on credit was not rife in the Fifties and still had its severe critics in the Sixties. Saving money for things that were desired was a thrifty and sensible method of acquisition. From clothes to holidays, to special treats the practice was to save: you can't have what you can't afford. Children saved their pocket money in saving stamps or in piggy banks. Adults were realistic about what their earnings could buy and few got themselves into needless debt by borrowing or overloading their budget.

46. Grandparents were older than in modern times. A grandparent under the age of forty was uncommon. The expectation would be to experience this second coming of parenthood in the sixth or even seventh decade of life and

again it was uncommon for great-grandparents to be around when a child was born. In many families today five generations exist in an overlapping period.

47. A box of matches was an essential item. From once being high on the shopping list its place is now redundant as almost all of the match's uses have vanished in time. Garden fires and coal fires have gone. The gas cooker now has a switch that emits a spark to light the gas. Both pipe smoking and cigarette smoking have declined and the lighter has taken the place of the match. For every thousand boxes of matches once sold in Britain, it is likely less than ten are sold today.

48. Door knobs were wooden. A twist of the wrist opened a door. The metal door handle, although an invention from the Nineteenth Century, didn't overwhelm Britain until the second half of the Twentieth Century.

49. A striking difference between the citizens of yesteryear and the people of today is in the ability to perform mental arithmetic. In an age without calculators and electronic tills, it was imperative to be able to perform mathematical tasks. Coinage was more complicated, weights and measures too. Education systems reflected this by a greater part of a school's syllabus being devoted to arithmetic. Everyone was confronted by numbers in one form or another and there were no technological devices to assist, thus the brain was put to use in a way that today's society doesn't demand with quite the same urgency.

50. Terry nappies once hung like huge white flags from every new mother's washing line. They were manufactured from a fabric that was able to absorb lots of water. There were

several ways of folding a nappy, and each mother had her method. The nappies were held on a child's rear with large pins. A single pin proved adequate for a small child when the nappy was folded triangularly, but two pins were best for a larger child if the nappy was folded in a rectangle. Nappy liners came along to reduce the stains after soiling, but when the age of disposable nappies arrived, Terry nappies almost disappeared into history.

51. The dishcloth which once graced every kitchen sink and was adapted for a dozen uses, primarily of course for cleaning dirty crockery, has given way to throw away scrubbing and cleaning products. What was once practical and useful is now thought unhygienic and their sales have decreased as a result.

52. The rates, which were an unpopular form of taxation based on the rentable value of a property, were eventually replaced by the poll tax under Margaret Thatcher's Government. However, unpopularity turned to riots in 1990 as the new tax became even more despised by homeowners. In 1993 the council tax replaced the poll tax.

53. Local dialects with their own unique words and phrases were plentiful in an age where the movement of peoples was infrequent. Fewer words were used in everyday life; there was little need for elaborate description and simple possessions needed few words for identification purposes. However, through all ages language evolves somewhat, and a steady flow of new words blended into English during the second half of the Twentieth Century. But as the ages of technology, media, transport, and people movement reached

peaks never before seen in human history new words flooded into the language as at an astonishing rate. Computers and their components brought a basket of fresh words, the young invented new words, foods from all continents added flavor to the language, and as the world shrunk by all things from all parts becoming accessible through one medium or another words from every corner of the world were absorbed into the English vocabulary. So overwhelmed by the huge changes in spoken English the old and the young had different understandings of many words by the century's end. Few of the older generation could keep pace with the rapid changes in language while to the young this vibrant new tongue was the inheritance they were born to speak. The movement of people, whether it was from country to country, or moving from their birthplaces within a country, were both factors in the decline of the local dialect and the personal expansion of vocabulary.

54. It is difficult to recall a business operating from behind locked doors in the post-war years for businessmen were in personal contact with their clients. Security, when people were working at their places of employment, was unthinkable. In some circumstances, there were checks when employees departed their workplaces. But as attitudes to safety, and the real fears or unjustified fears of robbery heightened, the entrances of workplaces became increasingly more secure. Employees locked inside buildings increased in number and those entering buildings were vetted by security officials or receptionists. The openness of many businesses suffered from restriction; the

trustworthiness of those within buildings and those who might enter a building became questionable. From an age of comparative innocence, we slid by degrees into the jaws of suspicion as the media told us what could happen as a consequence of our laxness.

55. The tank of water used to flush the toilet was some feet above the pot itself. To release the valve and release the water a chain was pulled. Usually, the chain had a wooden handle on its end. Still today elderly people may ask their grandchildren after they have been to the toilet, 'Have you pulled the chain?'

56. The city pavements were made from stone flags, of which a few still exist in old towns. Every child of the age at some time or another walked along the pavement without putting a foot on the gaps. Tarmac pavements eventually superseded them but they remain a fond memory of childhood to many.

57. Bakers sold biscuits from tins. There were different kinds of biscuits in each tin. The request from the housewife might be for 2lb of mixed, and they would be handed over the counter in a brown paper bag. Broken biscuits were sold at a lower rate.

58. In summer, the houses of the Fifties and Sixties were invaded by flies. Today it is unimaginable to believe so many of these insects could infest the home, but they were an unhealthy problem of the time. Before fly sprays were common a sticky fly strip was dangled from the ceiling to attract the insects. When they landed on it they were stuck and would die. They were dirty things but effective during their time of use.

59. Peddlers selling their wares were regulars at the door. Coal, watches, shoe polish, clothes, pegs, vegetables, cleaning materials, books, and almost any household requirement could be purchased from a peddler. A few that were dishonest gave others a suspect reputation, and by the early Sixties, the practice was declining. The variety of goods on the high street increased and peddlers had just about vanished by the end of the Seventies.

60. Most boys and a few girls collected marbles. They were sold in plastic bags in several shops and came in a whole array of colors. The usual game of marbles involved finding a hole in the road or pavement and deciding how many marbles each player would throw at the hole. Each player took it in turns to get the marbles in the hole. After a miss, the play was alternated. The player who got the final marble in the hole collected the whole pot.

61. Table manners were commonly practiced in the Fifties and early Sixties. As families ate regularly at the table instead of the more modern approach of being seated in a chair with a tray on the knee, manners were a customary bi-factor of dining. Children were told to sit straight at their seats, to close the mouth when eating, to not make rude noises, and to keep their elbows off the table surface. It was even deemed polite to remain at the table until all had finished the meal.

62. Before the days of boxer shorts and briefs, most British men wore Y-fronts as underwear. They were so-called because of the inverted Y of the seams. Although still manufactured

today the Y-front has been replaced as a market leader by more fashionable styles.

63. Many species of wild bird have been decreasing in numbers for decades. In the garden of yesteryear could be found finches, yellowhammers, warblers, sparrows, thrushes, magpies, starlings, doves, wood pigeons, robins, larks, swallows, martins, and many others. With the growth of the human population and the reduction in natural habitat came the rarity of seeing several breeds of birds daily. Pockets of these species exist, but they used to be plentiful throughout the land and they gave color to our everyday lives.

64. The attitude towards dogs entering shops has changed considerably. Once dog owners entered shops without concern. Over the closing decades of the Twentieth Century, thoughts changed and very few dogs are permitted in shops today. It is the prerogative of the shop owner whether he wishes to allow dogs on his premises, rather than it being an unlawful act to take them there. Hygiene is the main concern of all shopkeepers, especially those who trade in foodstuffs.

65. An iron in the Fifties was just that – a slab of iron. It was positioned on a tin plate on a coal fire, heated, and then used to iron clothes. When the iron cooled the process was repeated. They were dangerous appliances for there was no protection on the handle – it too was iron and a dampened rag needed to be used to prevent the hand from being scolded.

66. One of the most absurd aspects of life to a post-war child appeared on a visit to the dentists for a tooth extraction. A

child of this era was told all about the war years and how horrific they had been, especially for Jewish people who had been housed in concentration camps before being put to death by gassing. With this historical information in their minds, young impressionable children were seated in a dentist's chair and a gas-type rubber mask was strapped to their face. They were then knocked out by gas so the dentist may extract the tooth. Seldom has such barbarism been seen in modern times. The adult generation of the day should have realized that they were preparing new generations to be terrified of visiting the dentists.

67. In cities, the street bonfires on November 5th were popular occasions where neighbors gathered until late evenings. Lots of communities had a separate bonfire in each street. The early evening was supervised, but primarily for the kids. Later, adults would bring chairs from their kitchen and sit and drink around the burning embers. These social affairs grew less popular as organized park bonfires replaced them. They also became impracticable because motor cars began to clutter the streets.

68. Over the past sixty years, house prices have been on a helter-skelter ride from the earth to the sky. They rise and they dip, but as time passes their value is upwards. Of course, location is a primary factor, so too the size of the property and the surrounding land but as a generalization, house owners who may have been comparatively poor when they purchased a house many decades ago became considerably better off as a result of price rises. A Victorian terrace property in one of England's most pleasant cities which cost £600 in 1959 came

on the market in the first decade of the Twenty-first Century at almost £400,000. A three-bedroom semi in suburbia bought for £2,500 in 1971 reached £120,000 by 2010. Later still, a bungalow costing £21,000 in 1980 sod for £250,000 in 2013. These are just three examples, but there are millions more. The property owners of the past were fortunate when compared with the couples of modern times who struggle to save a deposit to gain a mortgage.

69. Few housewives would have been without a wooden clothes horse. Long before dryers, and even metal clothes hangers, the clothes horse was seldom out of use. It was made of two simple gate-type structures which had three slats each. They were bracketed together and opened to ninety degrees for the clothes to be draped over the slats. Commonly these devices could not accommodate the whole wash of clothes so when items were dry, other damp clothes took their place.

70. A sight to witness at coastal towns was the return of the fishing fleet with its accompanying chaos of seagulls overhead. So numerous were the boats that they filled an entire harbor. The piers were busy places and often the fish catches were sorted and sold in a building next to the harbor. There were activity and bustle aplenty, always an incident to entice the eye, and visitors from inshore towns and cities were entranced by the occasion. The depleted fleets of today do not attract the same attention and the fishing industry in Britain is on the wane.

71. The courtesy of a boy paying for a girl on a date has not wholly survived through the Twentieth Century. It was once unthinkable for the cost of a date to be shared. A fledgling

man had his pride and needed to impress his potential sweetheart with both his personality and his generosity: the female he hoped was destined to be his wife, the mother of his children, and his housekeeper. As women began to demand more from life during the closing decades of the century the man lost his power of being in charge. A suitor had to respect that she was as able as he, both in ambition and in financial matters.

72. Bread and butter pudding was an inexpensive dish that warmed kids in winter and satisfied their appetite. Few households had excess money for treats, and the pudding became a treat with very little cost. It was prepared by placing bread in a dish, adding both milk and butter, and then sprinkling sugar and currants over the top. The dish was placed in the oven until the protruding pieces of bread turned faintly brown. What a feast for hungry kids whose sweet tooth yearned for things other than vegetables.

73. Throughout the Industrial Revolution, there was a mass migration of people from the countryside to the growing cities of Britain. Agriculture, which had been the greatest source of employment through many ages, was giving way to manufacturing industries. Railways and mines created thousands of jobs. Village communities which had been dominated by the same few families for generations were losing their sons and daughter to the lure of the new city jobs. However, in many respects, the villages remained what they had always been – the homesteads of people who knew each other, whose families were comprised of an indigenous few mingled with a few from neighboring villages. As yet the

city-reared outsiders were a rarity. Not until the age of the motor car did the complexion of a village's population change. And by the close of the century, it had changed dramatically: for the first time in history, villagers had become minorities in their birthplace.

74. Public toilets were once a common feature in British towns and cities. A charge of 1d was levied on them which gave rise to the saying 'spend a penny'. During the third quarter of the Twentieth Century, a public convenience was never far away, but in the coming decades many were closed or demolished, and in modern times they are scarce, excepting at seaside resorts. It is likely that councils reducing their overheads, accepted hygiene standards, and acts of indecency contributed to their decline. It is also probable that because non -public buildings and large stores offered toilet facilities there was a reduced need for councils to sustain them.

75. Proverbs were part of everyday conversation in the middle of the Twentieth Century. Scarcely a day passed without hearing 'A bird in the hand is worth two in the bush', or 'You can lead a horse to water, but you can't make him drink'. These wise words along with dozens of other proverbs passed through the generations with the continuity of common sense in mind. But the rebellion of teenage youth in the Sixties shook off so many habits of the past and by the time their own children were born in the Eighties and Nineties, the proverb had fallen victim to language evolution. A user of proverbs today is likely to meet a blank response from generations that find metaphors incomprehensible.

76. Before 1961 it was a criminal act to commit or attempt to commit suicide. Those who attempted to end their own lives and failed could be imprisoned, so too, the relatives of those who succeeded. An Act of Parliament in this year decriminalized the act of suicide, and those who failed in an attempt no longer faced prosecution.

77. The humble potato nourished a majority of the British for well over 150 years. It was served boiled, roasted, and in later eras fried (chips). There is little doubt it provided the basis of a countrywide diet through many social changes and many sets of circumstances. Certainly, a majority of meals had potatoes as the main source of carbohydrates. The final decades of the Twentieth Century saw the intake of potatoes reduced. Other foodstuffs became popular substitutes. Rice and pasta were served with meals, and although the potato remains to this day a popular choice of shoppers it is not a compulsory purchase and many cooks have found alternatives to its once primary position on the meal plate.

78. The pets of bygone days would be envious of a present-day pet's diet. Pets were fed scraps, the leftovers of a family meal or any tit-bit it could find. The notion that a percentage of the family income might one day be spent on pet food would have been inconceivable to earlier generations. The best a dog could have hoped for is a bone from the butcher's shop, and even a cat might only be able to dream of a fish head.

79. Navy blue knickers were the order of the day for schoolgirls in the Sixties. The boys got a glimpse of them in physical education lessons. They were a stipulated item of a girl's

school uniform and became an unforgettable memory of a woman's past. In a few areas, the alternative was bottle green knickers that equally lacked the glamour of modern underwear.

80. Many houses of the post-war era were chilled by drafts. Through slate roofs, the wind roared and caused the upper house to be cold especially if no heating was available. Gusts rattled the windows and blew under ill-fitting doors. Full-length army blankets were hung from door frames to keep these drafts from the main room of the house. On the windows were thick heavy curtains that prevented cold permeating through other rooms. Double glazing, insulation, and central heating were years away for the average householder. Both they and their families were exposed to conditions that few Britons born after the Seventies have encountered.

81. The old rotary dial telephones, which preceded the touch-tone signaling system employed by phones of the Sixties onward, were not owned by a majority of householders. Indeed, the usual practice for those making a call was to visit the local phone box. Telephones were a luxury that working-class people couldn't afford, and as yet they had little use for them because scarcely anyone in their circle owned one. Business people in great numbers owned telephones long before the average man. It was probably long after the Sixties had ended, and in some areas, beyond the Seventies before chatting on the house phone became an ordinary part of life.

82. Spring-based beds and mattresses with springs were almost universal. They were the cheapest of available sleeping arrangements, though wooden slat bed bases too were not expensive. Poor quality products allowed the springs to break and to penetrate the surface of the mattress, so causing scratches to many a sleeper's body. When waterbeds, foam, and memory foam mattresses came to the fore as the century closed the end of the spring era was welcomed.

83. The modern supermarket with its thousands of square feet of shopping area and its car park which holds hundreds of vehicles is a vast enlargement of early self-service general stores that operated in Britain. Although the United States was quick to adopt the idea of self-shopping fewer than twenty stores were using this practice in England in 1947. It wasn't until the Sixties that supermarkets began adorning high streets, and even occupying large detached buildings constructed for other purposes. As the decades unfolded the supermarket chains grew bigger and this progress was reflected in the size of their stores. Specifically designed premises were built, the range of their goods increased greatly, and people in their droves flooded to them to find cheaper prices due to their ability to buy in mass. The supermarket buyers gained a tighter stranglehold on the market when they went directly to product manufacturers and growers; the former intermediaries in the purchasing process, the wholesalers, by degrees were bypassed.

84. Cobblestoned and setted streets survived well into the Sixties, and in some areas of historic interest still survive

today. They provided rather uneven surfaces for both horses and carriages of the past. but their advantages outweighed those of the dirt track in that they were resistant to weather and the traffic on them was heard. By the closing decades of the Twentieth Century the cobbles which once surfaced all Victorian terrace streets had been lost to more modern road surfaces such as tarmac and asphalt.

85. Bedsheets were accessories to everyone's bed. In winter thick sheets were used plentifully to keep sleepers warm. They were usually placed over the top of an inner cotton or nylon sheet which was smoother on the skin. Although the quilt has existed for centuries, the idea of a single quilt as a bedcover is relatively modern. Only in recent decades has the quilt replaced the bedsheet in a majority of British homes. As a result, less preparation is needed for a bed, and the management of a bed's laundry is much simpler.

86. Laundry was hung out to dry on washing lines by most people who had access to a garden or the width of a terraced street. Clothes were secured to the line by clip-shaped wooden pegs that were prone to snapping if they were pressed on too hard. It was a common sight in cities to see clothes blowing like lines of flags. Props generally supported the middle of the washing line, which if overladen, also became prone to snapping. Large metal hooks fixed to walls secured the line, and in gardens, many had clothes poles to which the line was tied. Toward the century's end the electric clothes dryer became ever-popular and today fewer people hang their clothes out to dry.

87. Football Pools began in the Twenties, and although they took a while to catch on they became the working man's weekly hope of fortune for many decades to come. The chief prize resulted from selecting eight matches that would end in a draw. Pools were either posted or handed to a local collector. Big winners of the football pools would often capture the newspaper headlines and they became regular topics of gossip. Players of this hope of wealth game reached a peak in 1994 when 10 million entries were received. However, that same year the National Lottery was introduced and from thenceforth numbers of players declined rapidly. The Lottery offered more lucrative jackpots and so replaced the Pools as the chief source of people's dreams of wealth.

88. The most obvious aspect of wages which has changed in the past fifty years is the transition from weekly pay to monthly pay. Most employees were paid weekly in the bulk of the Twentieth Century: this is not the case today. The gross income of workers has increased markedly, and a wage that once was swallowed by the expenses of food, clothing, and house costs is vastly more flexible. Any comparison of yesteryear's wage with one of today is meaningless, but what a worker can afford with the wage is more informative. From sparse and uncomfortable living conditions progress is striking. A wage in the Twenty-First Century affords what were once deemed luxuries. Transport, eating out, holidays, fashion, entertainment, gambling, unnecessary possessions, and celebrations are among today's ideas of necessities. It is

true to say that prosperity has come to all British people whatever their circumstances.

89. The nit nurse was a frequent visitor to primary schools throughout the last half of the Twentieth Century. Often nicknamed 'Nitty Nora the bug explorer' she would inspect children's hair, and if lice were discovered the child's parent would be sent the dreaded letter saying that their child was contaminated, and the hair needed treatment with lotion. However, as social values changed, it was thought to be intrusive for a stranger to explore a child's scalp, and further, the child found with nits may be subject to ridicule by classmates. The practice of the nit nurse died out in the Nineties, leaving parents with the sole responsibility of inspecting their children's heads for lice.

90. Inkwells had a place in school desks in the Fifties, and they were still in abundance in the next decade for children were taught to write with pen and ink. Fountain pens were widely used even though the biro was quickly overtaking them in sales. But in the course of a few years fountain pens fell from grace, they were thought messy and inconvenient. The inexpensive and efficient biro had sent the old fashioned method of writing into history by the middle of the Seventies.

91. There are conflicting theories as to why shops closed on Wednesday afternoons. Some have it related to the birth of Sheffield Wednesday Football Club, and others to an enterprising young man from Manchester who petitioned shop workers. Whatever, shops did indeed close for longer than today and even Sunday trading was prohibited. Before

1994 only garden centers, some specialist shops, and family-run corner shops were able to trade on the Sabbath. An attempt by the Thatcher Government of 1986 to change the law was defeated in parliament. Eventually, after large stores began to ignore trading laws a Sunday Trading Law was passed in 1994 which revolutionized shopping completely. The 24-hour store was not too far away.

92. A child of the past may have spent many hours in a meadow chasing butterflies, even capturing them in a net. There are two primary reasons for this seemingly innocent pursuit and of course the first relates to finding amusement. A child needed to be inventive because there weren't a plethora of toys available. But the second reason is that there were butterflies to catch. Together with ladybirds, greenflies, grasshoppers, wasps, and bees, they have significantly fallen in number from our greenfield surroundings. What was once a country teeming with life has become in great parts bereft of all life but that which is human.

93. In the post-war years, it was as common to hear men talking about county cricket as it was talking about football. The latest score in a match was interesting news. Even women recognized the names of cricketers who played for their particular county and there may be a modicum of pride felt if one of the local team was chosen to play for England. But again values changed society; cricket was a slow peaceful game spread over many hours and many days and it fell from favor. People demanded excitement, instant thrills, and plenty of noise. It wasn't until theTwenty20 version of

cricket, introduced in 2003, that the popularity of cricketers was revived.

94. The aroma of carbolic soap will be forever remembered by all school children of the pre-Seventies when its use largely died out. It smelled of disinfectant and was widely disliked by the young. Some children who used bad language in school were made to wash out their mouths with soap. Although the soap remains on sale it is not a popular choice of shoppers.

95. In the Fifties, the average woman who was not a full-time housewife could expect to work in a factory, a shop, in secretarial work, or the clothing industry; few opportunities existed for a woman to progress far in the world of employment. But attitudes changed speedily as the Sixties unfolded: women wanted more than to be domesticated baby producers, they wanted liberty and equality and the Sixties rebellion of youth assisted their cause. At the end of the next decade a woman, Mrs. Thatcher, became Prime Minister and proved an example to all women of what heights were achievable. The female of the species rapidly gained equality with men in most fields, and as the century came to an end, women had progressed to positions never thought within their grasp just half a century previously. It is clear today that women are capable of all jobs and that a male-dominated society is a notion of the past.

96. Many British people born in the early decades of the Twentieth Century never left these shores. Their entire lives were spent in one or two neighborhoods, occasionally traveling a short distance on trips or holidays, but the majority were certainly not travelers because they never had

the means and they never owned a suitable method of transport. Times changed slowly as holidays became affordable and the transport systems improved, but still, the glob-trotting British citizen was rare. However, when holiday packages which included accommodation and flights became widely available in the Sixties possibilities opened up for all people with incomes. Further, with car ownership, the distance became less of a problem. Not only did people start to broaden their outlook as to where to go, but they also found work was accessible further afield. By the end of the century, millions of Britons were traveling further in one year than their ancestors had traveled in a lifetime. What had once been a sedate nation of settled people became a busy population of traveling people.

97. The voting age which had been 21 years was reduced in the United Kingdom in 1970 to 18 years.

98. For hundreds of thousands of years, mankind roamed these islands in search of food and he gradually obtained new survival skills that furthered his path along the evolutionary trail. Somewhere along his journey, he took to horseback, and closer to our time he invented the boat, the bicycle, and the steam engine. Karl Benz is credited with inventing the first modern automobile in the late Nineteenth Century, and during the coming decades, many Europeans purchased their first motor cars. However, life for the ordinary working man was not radically changed by this series of progressions. Perhaps minor events illuminated odd days, even the occasional week in a year, but his life substantially was what it had been at any time in recent history. By the Fifties and

Sixties, all people were aware of the advance of the motor industry, but again, a majority of people had little or no experience of the car. However, car sales increased as earnings too increased, and we arrived at a point in the mid-Eighties when we had rush hour traffic in both the mornings and in the early evenings. As yet there were still many in Britain unfamiliar with driving and owning a car. Some people still viewed them as a hazard to crossing the road or as a nuisance taking space in front of their homes. We arrive at the close of the Twentieth Century and tiptoe into the Twenty-First Century: humankind encountered its greatest change since we climbed from the trees as primates. The cars had multiplied (there was mass ownership), they revolutionized the modern human's life as nothing had ever done before. Suddenly, a man had the whole earth in his sights. There was no limit as to how far he could travel by his own volition, in his own time, at great speed, and whenever he desired. He wasn't reliant on waiting for a bus, or a train, he wasn't restrained by set courses. The affordability of the motor car equalized the working man with his superiors and gave him possibilities to look further afield than he had ever previously envisaged. The car was a convenience unlike anything he had ever experienced and he possessed the means to seek adventure for both himself and his family like never before. What is more, he could carry things in them, he was able to personalize them, he could sell them, exchange them, park them, and even go for a drive and relax in them. An abundance of new problems, both pleasant and tedious came to affect his life. There were the expenses associated with taxing the car, insuring the car, maintaining the car, and buying petrol or diesel. And where did he keep the car – should he have a garage, a drive? Should he wash the car or take it to a car wash? Should he consider pollution and noise? Yes, in a few short years this machine which had been developed a century ago transformed the lives of millions and changed their lives completely. Many people today in a single hour see more cars than they do humans. They have negative aspects which include accidents and road deaths, and they tend to separate the driver from the people whom he once met on the walkways, but essentially the car is not only the creation that has shaped modern society it is also the accessory that has restructured the lives of millions of British people.

99. Before the widespread availability and use of the telephone, the telegram was the common method to send urgent news. In working-class society, those called on by the man in a blue uniform that carried a brown envelope were often thought to be the recipients of bad news for telegrams frequently told of death or something perturbing. A telegram was indeed a serious communication, but it was quicker than a letter in the post. To despatch a telegram the sender had to go to a post office with his message: each word was charged at a cost that kept the wordage to a minimum. Their use diminished with the advent of both e-mail and the telephone. By the late Sixties they were archaic, and very seldom used.

100.   The mangle was a piece of machinery used to wring water from washed clothes. The clothes were fed through two heavy rollers and water was squeezed from them by

turning a handle which was attached to cogs in the machine. Although mangles are still used for pressing garments, the invention of the spin dryer and the twin tub ended their use in the British home. Certainly, by the Seventies, few mangles were being used in conjunction with the old washing drums that washed the clothes.

101.   The T-shirt came into being as long ago as the Nineteenth Century when it was worn by miners and stevedores. In later times American navy sailors wore them, and in the Fifties, they were seen in films for the first time. However, the pop culture of the Sixties brought them to the fore and by the next decade, they were being personalized by the use of statements and slogans on their fronts. The popularity of the T-shirt has grown healthily and presently its place as the primary shirt wear for young people is uncontested.

102.   The scary 1d banger caused havoc on bonfire nights during the third quarter of the Twentieth Century. Used in mischief by children of the day they were available at an incredible 240 for one pound in the Sixties. However, safety considerations prevailed in the last quarter of the century and brought to an end the production of such notorious fireworks.

103.   Illegitimacy was once scorned upon and a young woman who had a child outside wedlock would be ostracised, or even banished from her community. The illegitimate children were often passed off as belonging to married family members, and in many families, secrets of children's births were kept from them. As easier attitudes

were adopted by society illegitimate births increased and mothers were no longer victimized. But still, the customary habit of having children inside wedlock persisted to the final two decades of the Twentieth Century. In 1980 only 12% of children were born to unmarried mothers in the United Kingdom; by 2007 the relentless ease of social attitudes resulted in a figure of 44%.

104.   Many word meanings changed dramatically during the Twentieth Century, none more so than 'gay', which was commonly used as meaning bright or showy, and is today predominantly used to describe the homosexual. 'Nice' used to mean hard to please, and 'decimate' referred to a reduction in number by one in ten. The youth of today have redefined the words 'wicked' and 'cool', and there are many new words that defy description by anyone born before the age of the internet. The tide of language forever flows but it has never flowed more rapidly than in present times.

105.   Once upon a time, helpful customers would take their used newspapers to the fish & chip shop for the benefit of the owner. The owner used the old papers to wrap customers' orders, and this practice continued for decades. When hygiene standards became more rigorous clean white or brown paper sheets replaced newspapers.

106.   Cut-throat razors were manufactured in Sheffield as long ago as the 1680s and their lifespan proved considerable. Until the first half of the Twentieth Century, they were the commonest method of shaving, and even though sales of them declined rapidly from the 1950s onward they have a tiny following today. The Gillette safety razor with its

replaceable blade was the first of its kind to outsell the cut-throat, and in the post-Fifties era, both electric razors and razors made from new materials came onto the market. The days of a man going to his barber for shaving by cut-throat are long gone in Britain and products associated with facial hair become more numerous and easier to use.

107.   There is great truth in the belief that people do not change, but it is the prevailing attitudes and conditioning of a society that changes their behavior, and how they exhibit their behavior. In the post-war world, youth was steered, if not controlled, by parental forces and the influence of the church. Sexual practices of the young were frowned upon, but it is human nature to explore sexual desire and the youth of the day were more secretive about their activities, and perhaps a little more fearful of practicing them than the young who were to inhabit the late Fifties. When the early pop stars came along and introduced youth to the possibilities of life, both with their lyrics and with their attractive vibrancy, the new culture of teenage-hood was born. Morality loosened its grip on sexual behavior, and as the Sixties dawned youth struggled free and demanded liberation including the freedom to choose what was permissible in life. Life was to be lived honestly and openly and if past generations condemned them for being themselves, unrestricted by what had gone on before, then so be it. However, the mythology of the Sixties being all 'drugs, sex & rock n' roll' is ridiculous. Because the pop culture exploded to new heights and was fuelled by an adoring youthful following, it was presumed that all young

people of this era were doing everything their idols were practicing. Sixties' youth certainly rebelled, but a majority still had morals, still respected many of the old values: their difference was largely in how these values were exhibited. The earlier secretiveness gave way to a refreshing openness which made them appear promiscuous beyond their actual promiscuity. Over the closing decades of the Twentieth Century youth increasingly became oblivious to what had previously been taboo. Contraception was freely available and young people had no compunction in using it, abortion statistic soared in England and Wales from around 30,000 cases in 1970 to around 190,000, 2010, and the number of mothers who bore children to different father's increased markedly – the state in an indirect way encouraging sexual freedom by financing the support of mothers with no earned income of their own. These latter points are not relative to youth, but they give some idea as to how values and habits have changed from the late Forties to the present time.

108.   The innocence of British society was shattered in the Sixties by at least two horrific series of child murders. The Moors Murders and the Cannock Chase Murders chilled parents as never before. Before these tragic events, it had been the custom for children to make their own way to school, or to be accompanied by other children. Very few parents were regularly seen at the school gate and the occasions they were asked to visit school were nothing to do with safety. It should be said that schools were local, and few pupils traveled far to their lessons, but the dangers of crossing roads were not the primary factor in a social change

that was so dramatic. By the Seventies, parents had begun taking children to school in vast numbers, especially primary aged children. This trend grew throughout the Twentieth Century and by its close, a majority of infants were accompanied on their journey by an adult.

109.	Wallpaper has drifted in and out of fashion over the decades, but the wallpaper purchased from the Sixties onwards differs from that which preceded it by way of borders. A roll of paper needed to be stripped of its edging before being used. This task was often done by two people; one person held the roll and the other carefully removed the edge which was approximately one-quarter of an inch wide at each side. Each edge had a perforated line to make its removal easier.

110.	One of the last major events watched in black and white on British television was the Football World Cup Final of 1966 in which England beat West Germany by 4-2. In 1967 color television was introduced.

111.	Generally, Sunday dinner was a more formal occasion than it is today; it was the primary meal of the week, and it was deemed necessary to appreciate such a luxury. The family would be seated in their best clothes at a table that had previously been set. The mother would hand out the meal to individuals and before eating grace was uttered by all. The words 'for what we are about to receive, may the Lord make us truly thankful. Amen,' was the customary verse. The meal was eaten regularly to a background noise of Family Favourites on the radio, which was a program that sent and received messages from servicemen working abroad.

112.   The pub was once a local institution prized by the bulk of society's vast army of drinkers. Cities had hundreds of them, no village was without one – pubs were the meeting places of people who wanted a drink and a chat, and this had been the custom throughout the ages. Although there are more drinkers today, and these drinkers consume more alcohol than ever before, fewer pubs are operating. Many factors conspired to reduce the number of pubs: health concerns about the over-use of alcohol contributed, so too, the smoking ban which applied to all public places from 2007. As long ago as the Seventies pubs were feeling the effect of competition from supermarkets and off-licenses who were able to offer products at cheaper prices. The pub suffered primarily from alternatives choices that had not existed to such an extent in the past. Bars and clubs, restaurants, and hotels served similar products and in the first decade of the Twenty-first Century, pubs were on a steep decline. Many in working-class areas closed, others adapted to the times and broadened their food businesses by offering meals and snacks.

113.   The duffle coat had its public heyday during the Fifties and the Sixties. Made from a duffel material they were worn by servicemen in both World Wars as an item of warm clothing. After World War II ended, they were sold as surplus military supplies until their private manufacture in the Fifties. Today, not so popular, they are made of Melton

cloth and thought to be a somewhat eccentric choice of clothing.

114.   Possessions have undergone radical changes through the course of six decades. From the cluttered homes of the past to the present sparseness of rooms, what people have owned has usually reflected the eras in which they lived. Several generations ago workers had little spare money and they relied to some measure on hand-me-downs from their parents: a second-hand sofa or chest of drawers, old crockery, and even former possessions of their grandparents were among their belongings. They had to make do with what was available, and few items were thrown away for one day they may come in useful. A little later, as new inventions became accessible and as wages rose, the old was steadily replaced by the new. People began collecting things, filling their homes with choices that were personal and which added comfort to their lives. But small luxuries were soon labeled necessities and life became a chase towards more expensive possessions. No longer was it wasteful to despatch the old in favor of the new, it was essential to do so. The rapid changes in technology had people spending money to keep up with the latest gadgets at whatever the cost. As the centuries turned the idea of cluttered homes had all but died, only the middle-aged and elderly clung to their possessions. Be it fashion or be it the latest mobile phone, younger generations needed to possess what was in vogue now. In several decades possessions that once were necessary to grasp and hold on to became the things that

must be got rid of, simply because new items had come along and it was without a point to keep old ones.

115.　　　Not only in life has destiny changed in modern times, but in death too. For centuries the dead were buried in graves. The first cremation in England took place at Woking in 1885, and the Cremation Act of 1902 formally legalized bodies being disposed of by this method. Burial remained the favored way of saying goodbye to the dead and it wasn't until after Pope Paul VI lifted the ban on cremation for Catholics in 1963 that cremation became as usual as burial. In 1960 on 35% of people in the United Kingdom were cremated; by 2008 that figure had risen to 72%.

116.　　　The centuries-old letter which once was the primary method of communication between people who lived distances apart is now the preserve of a minority. Before the telephone, the letter played a part in every literate person's life. Letter writing was an art in which some excelled, and in some cases on which fame was founded. A letter was a unique expression of thought and carried in great detail all aspects of the writer's life. Indeed, from letters of the past, historians gain their most revealing insights into the lives of their writers. It was something of a treat to receive a letter from a family member who had strayed to other parts and to read of their news and all the concomitant issues in their lives. Children at school were instructed in the art of letter writing and shown by example what a beautifully written letter could portray. Ordinary people were contributing daily to a record of human social history and they were leaving traces of existence which more modern methods of communication didn't so clearly describe. As telephones, mobile phones, computers, and e-mails proliferated, the letter failed by its lack of immediacy in a world which demanded all things at the present moment. The letter lives on, but its practitioners are few and its influence on the history of present times will be minimal.

117.   The Monday warm-up contained the remnants from Sunday dinner. Food was a more precious commodity in days when housewives had less money, and nothing was thrown away. A slight overuse of food on Sunday resulted in a 'free' meal on Monday; leftovers were heated in a frying pan and then served as a fresh meal. Sometimes an egg accompanied the warm-up which resembled a colorful slop comprised of potato and vegetables. Because it tended to be dry, a sauce often acted as a flavoring. The Monday warm-up has long gone but older generations still cherish its peculiarity.

118.   Twenty-eight tiny blocks of wood or ivory occupied the minds of millions of folks in leisure time during the decades preceding the Seventies. Dominos was a popular game, often played by old men in public houses. Each block was divided into two halves, and each half was blank or had one, two, three, four, five, or six dots. Matching halves were set against each value forming a long chain of blocks. The player that emptied his hand first was the winner. Many variations of the game existed, and although sets of dominos are still sold today it is not very commonly played.

119.   Grazed knees of boys are not a daily cause of concern for mothers as they were in the Fifties and the early to mid-

Sixties. The once frequent task of picking gravel from a child's skin, or bathing an injury in water laced with Dettol, has all but gone. The unsurprising culprit of this phenomenon was the short trouser which all junior schoolboys wore in this period. The hustle and bustle of the schoolyard resulted in many bleeding knees because the skin was not protected from the often rough surfaces of the ground. Short trousers for boys gradually lost favor, and with them went the need for a mother to inspect a boy's legs on his return home from school.

120. It is difficult to estimate what the money spent on a child's Christmas presents in this century would have bought for a child over six decades ago. The expectations of modern children could never have appeared the wildest dreams of their predecessors who, in large numbers could only look forward to waking on Christmas morning to a stocking filled with an apple, an orange, and a few nuts. Some children were given toys made by their father or grandfather, and more fortunate ones received a manufactured toy, but the contrast between these generations is staggering and highlights the significant rise in family incomes achieved in such a brief time-span.

121. The term 'old age pensioner' has given way to the more appropriate 'senior citizen': it was thought derogatory and widely disliked by the elderly. In part, this dislike of the term arose due to the diversity of people in the pensionable age group. Decades before fewer people lived long lives, and to classify the ones who survived into ripe old age as a single group was perhaps both appropriate and reasonably

matched to the attitudes of the time: an old person was distinctive, and so obviously identified by those younger. However, the older population swelled in the last decades of the Twentieth Century, and a vast majority did not exhibit the signs of decrepitude that had been associated with the aged. Men and women receiving pensions were undertaking activities never before associated with their age group; they were traveling, working voluntarily, exercising, taking up hobbies, and performing duties which had always been thought befitting only younger people. Today's senior citizens may well have one or two surviving parents. Social changes have brought greater comforts which themselves have lengthened the span of people's active lives.

122.　　　　The first two-ply toilet roll was produced at St. Andrew's Mill, Great Britain, in 1942. These rolls were softer than their predecessors and they marked a change in hygiene comfort. But working-class people were almost two decades from such luxury. In the Fifties, many water closets had simply a metal hook on which torn sheets of newspaper were slotted. Not only did men read the newspaper whilst sitting on the toilet, but they also used it for hygiene purposes. Izal medicated toilet tissues, with their distinctive green and white wrapper with red-lettered product name became popular in the Sixties. In the coming decades, the quality of the rolls improved, and the variety of brands broadened.

123.　　　　Both the Industrial Revolution and the Age of Mining altered the landscape of Britain. The creation of cities, railway systems, and canals halted nature in its tracks, and slags heaps had man changing the natural design of landscapes as never before. But none of man's pursuits altered the complexion of his homeland like the construction of roads. From the relatively idyllic terrain of the Twentieth Century's first half sprung the chaotic network of road systems that scars the landscape of the early Twenty-first Century. The Special Roads Act of 1949 paved the way for all that was to come, and in the early Fifties, the government gave the go-ahead for the construction of new roads. The first piece of motorway, the Preston Bypass in Lancashire opened in 1958, and this was quickly followed by the first full-length motorway, the M1, the very next year. A ceaseless program of road-building saw the first 1,000 miles of motorway completed in 1972 and between 1985 and 1995 the road network expanded by some 24,000 miles. Roads devoured land as traffic swelled to fill them. Ancient sites of meadows, farms, crop fields, woods, and forests fell to the relentless bulldozer of progress. Roads were widened, extended, upgraded to motorways. Bypasses were built, bridges erected, and enormous junctions that consumed as much land as a small town were born from the sweat of the road builder. England's green and pleasant land became a criss-cross of grey tarmacadam; few areas escaped man's desire to commute faster and to reach his destination by the shortest route.

124.	The Yale door lock secured many doors in the Fifties and Sixties and was responsible for thousands of people being locked out of their homes. If the latch of the lock hadn't been placed in the closed position a door was liable to swing and shut out the homeowner. Hence the saying 'Put the latch on'. Yale locks usually had a small brass key and the lock was positioned about two-thirds the height of a door. They were very common in terrace houses, but they proved less robust than locks that replaced them. Few remain due to security concerns of today's householders but they left an amusing catalog of stories from those who experienced their quirkiness.

125.   The focal point in classrooms of the past was the blackboard on which a teacher wrote related lesson matter in white chalk. Strangely, a blackboard was seldom black: it was grey due to the layers of rubbed out chalk from past lessons. Often a class monitor had the specific job of rubbing the blackboard. They had a narrow grooved ledge beneath them on which the teacher placed his chalk sticks. Blackboards survive but only in limited numbers inside schools: teaching methods have changed and so to the layout of many current-day rooms in which children are educated.

126.   Social history can make a mockery of statistics and in many ways provides a more realistic assessment of ages than facts construed from figures. A look at average weekly wages from the period 1950 to 2000 tells us that the average worker earned £7.08 in 1950, £13.69 in 1960, £26.10 in 1970, £111.20 in 1980, £263.10 in 1990, and £419.70 in 2000. These figures do not reflect the truth of segmented parts of society. The average weekly income of a solicitor, a member of parliament, and an office cleaner may well exceed £2,000 today but this figure is likely to be ten or even fifteen times the office cleaner's weekly wage. There are tens of thousands of shop workers presently in employment who do

not earn the 1990 average income of £263.10. Society, like it or not, is separated into various income brackets – those with menial jobs can't have incomes in any way comparable to those of professionals. For the purposed of this book, it is suggested that the quoted average incomes above should be almost halved in the case of working-class employees, remain similar for the middle-classes, and be at least doubled or trebled for higher earners. An important factor too when considering the incomes from any period should be not in the substance of the income, but the purchasing power of the income in each specific period.

127.   Punishments inflicted by parents, schools, and societies have been barbaric in most ages and it wasn't until the Nineteenth Century that opposition to corporal punishment gained strength. The 1948 Criminal Justice Act finally ended whipping and flogging in Britain (with certain exclusions) but it did not prevent physical punishment by other means. In the homes of the Fifties and Sixties, the brutality of fathers persisted, for they too had been brutalized as children and they saw it as the way that children should be reared. Children received the belt or a slap as punishment for misdemeanors. The cane or some other implement was widely used in schools and even in society it was accepted that a policeman might give an errant child a clip round the ear. The notion that it was wrong to hit children had not yet gained universal agreement. Though social reformers were shouting not everyone listened. Public opinion eventually swayed and by the Eighties, the cane was rarely used. Better parenting, the Human Rights Act, and a

change in attitude to violence disallowed anything other than a tap or a light smack being administered to children. In half a century the cruel nature of modern humans was tamed: the beating of a child today is a heinous crime punishable by many years in jail.

128.	Between World War I and World War II four million new suburban homes were built in Britain making it the most suburbanized place in the world. One million of these new houses were built by local authorities who attempted to house families in decent dwelling places with their own gardens. A feature of these properties was the privet-hedge-lined front garden which promised greenery that was manageable. Until the final decades of the Twentieth Century, the privet hedge reigned supreme on the borders of council house gardens. It could be determined how orderly or how unruly a tenant lived within his society by the neatness or ruggedness of his privet border. A privet hedge was a badge of decency or a sign of carelessness. But as drives became a convenience for the car and as sales of council houses grew, the humble privet hedge began to lose its popularity. Today many streets have but a few or none at all, and those which still exist are usually well maintained.

129.	Jockeys have grown in stature and increased in weight over the past fifty years. Once, tiny men who regularly weighed much less than 8 stones, they are now taller and able to ride with more bodyweight. Today there are female jockeys too who frequently ride winning mounts.

130.	The transistor radio became the most fashionable hand-held accessory of the Swinging Sixties. From a previous era of hardship and war sprung three dynamic forces which would come together and make the transistor the in-thing for short period. A post-war baby boom created a vast amount of Sixties teenagers and for the first time, teenagers had disposable income chiefly as a result of their parents' improved living standards. This new comparatively wealthy army aligned to the rise of popular music made the transistor a must-have item. Thousands of different transistors were available, but as the Seventies got underway new gadgets were invented and the sales of a once supreme social accessory went into decline.

131.　　　A society by definition has a distinctive culture and shared institutions that govern it; the individuals of a society are related to each other through persistent relationships. The news of yesteryear reflected this with the release of localized information. It was more interesting to learn of what was happening in the society in which individuals lived than to hear of occurrences in distant lands that had no effect on people's lives. Foreign news was sparse, the world seemed a massive place to the ordinary citizen and few of them cared what was happening in places outside their own country. Local newspapers were exceedingly popular and reflected what people wanted to learn about. National news headlines were dominated by events that were British based: few foreign events were deemed notable enough to break this trend. But as decades unfolded and countries became increasingly internationalized, and travel was made easier, news correspondents departed to all corners of the globe. The knowledge base of people broadened and they acquired an appetite for the learning of global concerns and worldly happenings. The mildly stirring stories of the past were displaced by major disasters and important stories from abroad; they were listed as secondary news items or disappeared from bulletins altogether. Today there is a greater balance of news and the modern citizen is far more aware of what is happening in a world that shrinks by degrees of invention and communication.

132.   Few things came instantly to people of the past: patience and planning were bywords for obtaining possessions or progressions. 'All things come to those who wait' was a saying of past generations. With instant food, instant shopping, instant credit, instant cash, and immediate technology, the needs of people today are satiated by methods never previously available. Today the notion of waiting for things is anathema to many.

133.   Schoolgirls of past generations were expert ball jugglers. Their playtime game, often taken to the streets, involved keeping two, three, four, or even five balls up in the air by skillful dexterity of the hands. Some girls were so good at it that they used only one hand. The same game could be played using the surface of a wall. Many schoolboys tried to emulate their achievements, but most boys were unable to juggle two balls successfully.

134.   The wooden tennis racket used by every professional player decades ago is now obsolete. Although the metal tennis racket was around in the Twenties it wasn't until 1969 that Wimbledon was won with an aluminum racket. Wooden rackets lost favor with players and throughout the Seventies

use of the metal racket boomed. The swansong of the wooden racket came at Wimbledon in 1981 when players using it won both major finals.

135.   A respectful society emerged from the debris of World War II in which the long-held tradition of addressing people by their titles continued. The frequency of use of the addresses Mr and Mrs was as common as in past generations. This titling, even of neighbors, was not presumed formal but deemed a respectful way to refer to those who were not relatives or close friends. This attitude prevailed in workplaces, especially in non-physical jobs, and it certainly applied in workplaces to superiors in all spheres. In schools, teachers were addressed as Sir or Miss, and children were addressed solely by their surnames. The use of the Christian name did not arrive swiftly or universally during the coming decades, it was an imperceptible social change that crept in by tiny fractures in what was judged respectable. But the change did occur and one of the last groups to publicly acknowledge this new practice was the politicians. If any single leader influenced this change it is probably creditable to Tony Blair whose informal style seemed to relax attitudes to propriety.

136.   From the health-conscious society of the Twenty-first Century's second decade, it is difficult to understand a world where smoking on wards in hospitals by both visitors and patients was commonplace, where the top deck of a public bus was clouded by the fog of smoke, where smokers continued their habit in shops, where tab ends were noticeable street rubbish, and in which around 40% of adults

puffed away in the presence of children. The Smoker once a socially normal member of society is now a pariah to many: few public habits such as smoking have taken such a battering. From the Fifties, the link between smoking and cancer was widely known but it took a further thirty years before the public conscience responded to this information. The Eighties saw smoking decline in Britain and as the habit continued to be publicly vilified by health professionals and other prominent members of society a range of measures to dissuade smokers from their habit were put in place. The early Twenty-first Century possessed almost as many former smokers as those who continued to smoke, and every year that passes gains adherents to a new healthier lifestyle than that which prevailed fifty years ago.

137.   Few remnants from the past are remembered with such fond recollections as the coal fire. Once present in most British homes the idyllic scene of a family huddled around a hearth being warmed by a flaming fire is legendary, but the truth of many coal fires is much different. Even the preparation for a fire was a dirty business. The ashes from the previous evening's blaze first had to be removed; usually taken from beneath the grate in a pan which overflowed with fine ash and the slightest movement whilst carrying it resulted in spillage. The fire was set with paper and laid over with kindling covered by coal. Often the lighting of the fire proved unsuccessful; fresh paper needed to be used and the fire had to be relit. There was no instant warmth: it could take over half an hour before the fire started glowing, and even when laden with hot glowing ashes the heat from the

fire warmed only the front of those around it – very much like standing at a bonfire on a cold November night. Coal was kept in a cellar, or a shed or coal bunker outdoors. It was brought into the house in a scuttle which usually had a place at the hearthside. On the hearth, a companion set which contained a brush, small shovel, tongs, and poker was placed. The fire would belch out smoke, there would be cinder falls, soot falls, the fire had to be poked to allow it to breathe, and the grate had to be constantly opened or closed to let oxygen to the fire when its glow dimmed. Nothing done in the house in the past century created as much filth as the coal fire. Nothing in our environment stained it so much. Indeed, a feature of city houses of this period was bricks blackened by soot: smoke damaged people's respiratory systems and caused their clothes to smell. By the Sixties, gas fires were being installed in many homes, and in the Seventies, the age of coal as the major source of fuel was being seriously challenged. With mines becoming uneconomical and the new expectations of a cleaner environment coal fires rapidly diminished in number during the final decades of the century. The comparatively clean air in today's cities was no such luxuries to those living in earlier times.

138.   Before hot water became instantly available from the tap children were washed with soap and flannel. Mother filled a bowl with warm water, lathered the flannel with soap, and proceeded to scrub the child's hands and face. Many children from the Fifties and Sixties will remember soap going up the nostrils or in the eyes. The flannel was

rinsed to wipe away the soap. Today sponges are popular, and other cleaning accessories, but the flannel once lead the way in washing children.

139.　　　In a modern world where both education and information are freely available to a majority, there is scant reason for unfounded beliefs to exist to such an extent as they did in the past. Much of yesteryear's intelligence was passed down through the generations and habits were not frequently changing because conformity ruled the day. Beliefs were a great part of this dubious intelligence and stories that bolstered a belief were widely told. The primary belief that prevailed in Britain was that a god existed, and it followed that a god watched over people and noted their behavior: good would be rewarded and sins would be punished. A belief in the afterlife sustained the belief in heaven and hell. Of course, hell necessitated the existence of a devil that in turn was to be feared. There were fears too of demons, ghouls, unknown forces, and of ghosts. The belief in the soul or the spirit was strong too, and from an incident early in the Twentieth Century, there were still those who believed in fairies. But major forces combined to continue Darwin's work of the Nineteenth Century: two World Wars dented a belief system that had already been damaged by the theory of evolution, the rebellion of Sixties' youth brought a wave of new thinking, and primarily both education and technology developed to an extent that all people began to question that which previous generations had believed to be true or false. By the close of the century, more people in Britain were without a belief than ever before and children were minded to form their own views of existence.

140.   Devices of the recent past had buttons. They were turned on by a switch or a button. The remote control did not exist in most homes until after the Seventies, and it wasn't until the Twenty-first Century began that it became common to operate several devices remotely.

141.   Before cereals and snacks were available in multiple choices children happily munched on buttered toast, jam sandwiches, and dripping and bread. These cheap sources of nourishment furnished many working-class tables of the mid-Twentieth Century. Toast has never lost its appeal, and there are many more varieties of jam today than in past times but dripping and bread took a beating from health-conscious parents who today are disinclined to feed their offspring unnecessary fat content in their food.

142.   Hopscotch remained a favorite game of schoolgirls until the final decades of the Twentieth Century. A grid drawn on the ground had rising numbers written on each square. A girl threw a stone on each succeeding number until she has hopped the full length of the grid, without placing a foot in the occupied square, and returned to the starting point. It was one of those meaningless games which boys didn't understand and scarcely if ever, attempted to play.

143.   Shopping catalogs, or club books as they were commonly known, gave housewives a means of buying goods by a weekly payment plan. A 1950s woman could purchase items chosen from the catalog and pay for them over 20 or

38 weeks. Many women became agents and passed their books to family and friends so they too could make purchases. An agent was paid a small commission which both encouraged her to both sell and buy more goods from the catalog. This method of shopping proved popular until the widespread availability of credit and the variety of goods offered on the high street brought about its steady decline after the Seventies. From 1990 catalog shopping declined more rapidly as a result of internet shopping.

144.   The growth of population in the United Kingdom during the past sixty years has been constant, rising approximately by around 2 million in each decade. From a 1951 50.2 million people to 52.8 in 1961, 55.9 in 1971, 56.3 in 1981, 57.4 in 1991, and 59.1 in 2001 to 63.1 in 2011 a 26% increase in population can be determined. Statistics give us more evidence of the origins of people dwelling in the United Kingdom and what proportion of them are white British, but as these islands' past is a history of influxes of peoples from near and distant places these figures can be interpreted in different ways. The questions of what is defined as white British or what is the true population of these islands are as much related to personal opinion as they are to statistics. There can scarcely be a family whose history includes only British born people if that history is traced back to several generations. Population statistics rely on numbers that are counted, and as all people are not counted, these interpretations too are not accurate. The evidence of personal experience over sixty years is far more compelling and by contrasting scenes from the past with present ones

gives a clearer picture of both rates of immigration and population growth. In the Fifties and Sixties, non-white British were generally clearly defined by either their skin coloring or by their language and their mode of dress. Because foreigners were fewer, they were easily identified, and more likely to be discriminated against. By contrast, today huge communities of immigrants, especially in city areas, are vibrant parts of society. Where once it was so clear as what constituted British, today a British scene of society can contain any mixture of peoples and races from just about anywhere in the world. The length and breadth of Britain are filled with multicultural communities that are as much British as the scenes from yesteryear. And if it is to be accepted that the statistical record of there being merely 50.2 million people in Britain in 1951 when the evidence of the eyes revealed that villages were tiny, towns were small, and cities had boundaries, then today it is evident that the population is far greater. Villages have swelled to the size of towns; some towns are indeed small cities, and cities have swollen to overflow land that was formerly countryside. The growth of population to 63.1 million in 2011 is indeed dubious: a figure greatly above this would appear to be more accurate.

145.   The fashion of floor covering has changed in recent decades from the ever-present carpet to wooden flooring. Wood bases are easier to clean and they contain less hidden dirt than the carpet. Certainly, for four to five decades the carpet proved the choice of most householders but in the 1950s working-class family carpets were a luxury. Many

homes had linoleum on the floors with perhaps the luxury of small mats in the best room and the master bedroom. Throughout the Sixties carpets became affordable but linoleum was retained in hallways and kitchens. Ironically, today linoleum is as expensive as carpet but both have lost sales to the modern wooden floor.

146.   Penny slot machines filled the sea-side arcades of both the Fifties and Sixties: they were mechanical gadgets that offered prizes of sixpence or more. A whole range of ingenious ways for a penny to give entertainment existed, from a clown that laughed to the lighting of small bulbs in a row. Decimalization in the early Seventies caused machines to be upgraded and reinvented. Largely 2p machines replaced them and more advanced machines powered by electricity hastened the demise of the old machines. More recently technology has played its part and today computer chips regulate play on machines which offer a year's salary of the 1950s worker as the top prize.

147.   Two stark differences between modern cities and those of the post-war era are night-time noise and the illumination of darkness. It is common today to see people through every hour of the night: they talk, they make sounds with footsteps, they drive cars and some are awake in their homes with noise seeping out of windows. Every street is illuminated, so too, every road and a majority of large buildings. The cities of the past were quiet and in many areas in darkness. Often the stillness of the night was a mirror of that found in the countryside and the only noises were whispers of the wind.

148. Sweet shops were a feature on shopping parades before parents became more conscious of the effects of sugar concerning tooth decay. The shops displayed large glass jars filled with assorted sweets. Quantities, usually of 2oz or 4oz, were wrapped in plain white bags and sold to customers who had requested a particular sweet. But steadily these specialist shops became victims of both newsagents who also sold sweets, and of supermarkets.

149. A popular pastime that occupied many winter evenings before blanket television was solving jigsaw puzzles. A huge board could be found in many houses on which the jigsaw was set. With 500 and 1000 piece puzzles, there was insufficient time for their completion on the dining table between meals. Most family members fixed a piece or two until the finished jigsaw was looked over by all.

150. A great many families of the 1950s were much the same as they had been for generations: most family members lived close to each other, family members traveled short distances to employment, their new relationships were formed with locals, and when they fled the nest their new homes were locally positioned. However, human progress conspired to change this culture radically over the coming decades, and by the close of the century, it was more common to find family dispersal than to identify families huddled together. Transport first made it possible to search for and to accept employment in distant areas. Public transport systems and cars allowed people to explore new surroundings, and even settle in them. Jobs once impossible to commute to now attracted potential employees from a

wider catchment area. Consequently, people met strangers and formed relationships never previously considered. As social values changed and individual wealth increased it became possible to educate more young at universities, to progress through the housing market, to journey to foreign parts, and even to divorce a partner and have a new family with another partner. The family as it had been known, and which had been the building block of society, became more like a spider's web whose dimension was limitless. Technology contributed too to this dispersal. The internet allowed the most distant family members to keep in touch: what had been the other side of the world to a family of the Fifties was now a click away. Inside half a century invention by degrees reshaped every family in Britain.

151.   As in the cases of both immigration and population, the statistics related to church attendance do not fit comfortably with life experience. In the post-war years, most churches had healthy congregations that on Sunday could be seen flooding from the doors when a service ended. The serving vicar, standing at the exit, often shook each hand as individuals departed. In those days it was rare to walk through several streets without seeing a church: they were numerous and well maintained. But as early as the 1960s many churches became victims of falling attendances. Churches closed, were turned into warehouses, shops, and converted into homes or flats. Throughout the remaining decades of the Twentieth Century, there were considerable closures due to the tide that flowed against belief and religion in general. Even the minority of churches that

survived this long period of decline did not see increased attendances, and still today many struggle to survive. The evidence of life experience suggests that church-going, although alive in some communities, is massively not as popular as sixty years past. Should this decline continue it is unlikely churches as we presently know them will be around in the mid-Twenty-first Century.

152.   A pre-1960s hairdresser's or barber's shop was unlikely to cater for both males and females. However, as men grew their hair longer in the Swinging Sixties unisex hairdressers appeared on the high street. Their popularity increased in the Seventies and today it is common practice for males and females to visit the same establishment for a haircut.

153.   In the early days of popular music, the 78rpm vinyl disc was king. But from the late Fifties onward technology progressed swiftly and the 78s gave way to 45s (used usually for single songs on each side) and 33s (long-playing records with approximately six songs on each side). But at the dawn of the Seventies, the cassette came along to challenge these vinyl discs on the market place and by the end of the decade, vinyl was quickly falling from fashion. However, the cassette too was quickly challenged as the CD (compact disc) took off in the Eighties. In later times more methods of listening to music and ways of storing music became available, and even though both the CD and the vinyl still sell it is doubtless that this relentless rate of change will continue for years to come.

154.   What can be thought of as slightly surprising about the past sixty years is the relatively unchanged nature of an

average home's layout. Open-plan houses are indeed favored by a minority, and en-suite bathrooms have become a trend, but on the whole, the modern house is basically the same as it was in the past. The kitchen, dining room and living rooms are downstairs whilst the bedrooms are upstairs.

155.   New clothes could not be easily afforded from the wages of a working man in the Fifties. Children frequently wore hand-me-downs which older siblings had outgrown, and the mother of the house had her prize sewing box at hand for damaged clothes that needed attention. All girls were taught the crafts of sewing, darning, and knitting. Sewing needles came in various sizes and were used with cotton of varying thickness and strength. Larger repairs were performed with darning needles and wool. A mother kept many balls of wool in different colors. In her sewing box would be a tin of buttons and other odds and ends to keep clothes useable. It was also cheaper to knit clothes than to buy new ones. Knitting patterns were sold in shops and printed in magazines. Knitting was widely practiced by many females and experienced hands were able to ply their craft at astonishing speeds and produce superb garments.

156.   A road in the third quarter of the Twentieth Century was for the most part a long grey strip of land on which cars traveled – perhaps with a central broken white line, but little else. By comparison, today's roads and highways are painted canvases; they are overloaded with lines both white and yellow, dotted lines, unbroken lines, double or single lines, in grid formations, in curves and circles, in arrows, directions,

words, numbers, spots, dots, chevrons, humps, solid blocks, instructions, and zones. They would prove a source of confusion for the driver of the past and it is a testament to the abilities of modern drivers that they can traverse these highways with fewer fatalities than resulted on the uncluttered and simple byways of yesterday.

157.   The role of women changed greatly in the second half of the Twentieth Century. In the 1950s most married women were housewives who looked after the home and children as the man of the house earned money at his workplace. By the Sixties, more women started to pursue careers which led to the desire for female equality in the 1970s. Women were better educated than ever before and careers once totally dominated by men opened their doors to the female sex. Throughout the closing decades of the century as expectations of people grew increasingly more women took to the workplace to give families two incomes. It is likely today that both parents work in some capacity, and equally likely that the woman has parity in wages with the man.

158.   There has been a major shift in awareness among people in recent history. Where once the bulk of knowledge was gained from local sources and related to the community in which people lived, today knowledge springs from a multitude of sources. People of the past had some fears, but these fears largely related to financial problems, health matters, ensuring their children didn't have accidents and minor issues that may affect their family or their social status. Their fears were based on the reality of their

surroundings and for the most part, any concerns were founded. The explosion of news and the tendency the modern world has for pointing out what may happen as opposed to what is likely to happen has caused people of today to harbor a whole host of unreasonable fears. Stories of disaster, tragedy, crime, and everything bad circulate with immediacy and seduced people into thinking that nothing is beyond their doorstep. The citizen of today might fear pedophiles, rapists, terrorist, murderers, robbers, arsonists, fraudsters, embezzlers, muggers, bombs, guns, air crashes, the mentally disturbed, man-eating sharks, venomous spiders, kidnappers, burglars, car thieves, cancers, and other diseases, and a hundred other nasty subjects which have been covered in news stories. These subjects are discussed with real feeling, and it is common for a child to be kept indoors because of a parent's fears. There is no doubt that everyone should be mindful of dangers in society but an unrealistic view of fears impedes a healthier attitude towards physical freedom. Surprisingly, the motor car, which should be the number one fear for it still causes the deaths of thousands each year, is low on the list. This contrast of people living only fifty years apart highlights how media growth has altered the average person's perception of the world.

159.   City pollution is a major success story for modern Britain. The once smoke and soot infested cities of the pre-Seventies gave way to the fume infested cities of the late Twentieth Century period. However, a reduction in car gas emissions brought cleaner air to city streets, and with an

active program from Blair's Government to make cities better places to live the transformation was visible by 2005.

160.   The humble doorstep seems an unlikely entry but in both the Fifties and Sixties it was a carefully tended object. Women kept their doorsteps clean and scrubbed. It was the entry point to terrace homes and sometimes painted or colored with stone. Even the near pavement received a wash with a broom and a mop and many women judged other women's cleanliness by their doorsteps.

161.   Local evening newspapers carried a special column for jumble sales and the many which took place were advertised here. On Friday evenings and Saturday afternoon's the church hall was the place to go to find a bargain. The sales had both clothes and bric-a-brac and were busy affairs that produced incomes that contributed to the upkeep of churches. Other institutions like the boy scouts or local halls also held sales. Great crowds, mainly of women would rifle through piles of clothes in a hurry to find a special bargain that would fit a family member. These popular events only declined as incomes grew and clothes became less expensive.

162.   Car parks seldom entered the mind of an ordinary 1950s citizen and ten years on things hadn't changed much at all. For the car owner, there was space to park wherever he went for fewer cars were on the road. But throughout the Sixties car ownership increased dramatically and the need for car parks became apparent. In cities, at workplaces, at the sea-side and large shops there existed insufficient slots for car parking. Over the coming decades, the awareness of a

need for parking places shaped building programs and the entire suburban landscape. From housing developments to shopping centers and places of employment the car had to be considered. Is it usual in modern times for a car park to be larger than the place it serves and this is hardly surprising when over 30,000,000 cars were on British roads by 2010. If an average car needs the space of an average room to park in (around 20sq.meters.) then these 30,000,000 vehicles will require 600,000,000sq.meters of space which is approximately 232 square miles of Britain's green and pleasant land.

163.   In former times most parades of shops could boast a greengrocer's where housewives bought fruit and vegetables for the family diet. Many large towns and cities had a wholesale fruit and vegetable market which supplied these shops. But as the buying power of the supermarkets grew throughout the Seventies and Eighties, wholesalers found their role as middlemen losing their place in the buying chain. Greengrocers could not compete with cheap supermarket prices, and they began to lose trade. Some greengrocers have survived but their numbers are greatly reduced and the once vibrant fruit and vegetable wholesale markets have almost disintegrated.

164.   The plimsoll served as footwear for children and young adults who were sporty in the Fifties and Sixties. There was the boot for football and rugby, and shoes for cricket, but little else. As sport diversified and its image became glamorized the once boring black or white plimsoll gradually evolved into a modern trainer with its array of

designs and bright colors. Its comfort was recognized by the general public and millions of people forsook the shoe in favor of the trainer for daily wear. Trainers became a fashion status and branded names were desired by youth. All generations found them convenient and easy to wear and by the Twenty-first Century the shoe was no longer the most popular footwear.

165.　　　Relationships between men and women have undergone a steady but significant change over the past six or seven decades. The virtues of marriage have been rejected by millions of couples who today set up a home together without the need for a formal contract or a public commitment to vows. Marriage was the institution favored by most Fifties and Sixties partnerships of a man and a woman. It was seen as the bedrock of society and the normal foundation on which to rear children. Many couples who married in this era were committing to their first loves, just as their parent had done before. 'Living in sin' was not wholly acceptable and was still not thought a decent association that should include children. However, many factors combined in the second part of the century that radically altered the belief that a partner was for life. The beginnings of this change probably lie with the emancipation of the Sixties youth but so many shifts in social attitudes can be mentioned. The man, who had held his power and his status as ruler of the home for centuries was at last challenged by a woman. She could no longer be dominated or brutalized as in past generations, she gained equality in law and had possession of her own finances. Women were able to end relationships in the same way as men. And their bolder attitudes ensured they wouldn't shirk from finding another partner. The new age of looser morals didn't restrict them, didn't stigmatize them to an extent that they would end up lonely spinsters. And as the century progressed the stigma once attached to the unmarried mother also dissipated. Relationships, like everything else, lasted only as long as they were rosy – no longer. The fast-moving world was reflected in the attitudes of people to each other. By the Eighties children of parents who were teenagers of the Sixties were bearing children and the idea of what couples ought to do if setting up home together was not clearly defined: options existed, ranging from total commitment to 'move in today and to hell with tomorrow'. People did not have to endure tough times as in the past, escape routes were available and one of these was that someone more appealing might come along. After all more places to socialize meant more members of the opposite sex to see, fresh faces to meet, better dressed, and wealthier potential partners than ever before. If the celebrities of the day could live in the fast lane then surely their followers were entitled to the same privilege. Of course, many couples retained old values and society is not a cesspit of debauchery, but in general, the shift has been to less enduring relationships and a greater number of partners. Personal choice prevails over moral and social choice which results in people of today seeking happiness rather than being resigned to their fate. Perhaps there are more victims of this new society but there are also fewer people willing to accept that both circumstance and fortune can't be improved.

166.   Savory ducks fed many a hungry child in the mid-Twentieth Century. Sold by butchers as a cheap alternative to meat poorer mothers served fried slices to their kids to warm them in winter. Some over fifties remember them fondly but others cringe at the very thought of eating savory ducks again.

167.   Most local communities were visited by an annual fair which was usually set up on the same site at the same time of year. Fairs attracted hundreds of people who sought the thrill of fairground rides or the chance of winning a prize from a stall. Young men took their girlfriends and mums and dads took their children for an evening of entertainment, unlike anything that normally occupied their lives. There are still traveling fairs today but their attraction has less appeal to generations who possess a far greater choice of amusements.

168.   Three significant periods make up the years from the 1950s to the present time: the Age of God & Morality, the Emancipation of Youth, and the Quest for Wealth. During the first period, the people of Britain were stuck in an orderly system that had their social status rigidly defined and they tended to accept the rules that governed their existence. Both religion and morality served to keep them in check and few from working-class backgrounds dreamed of venturing further up the social ladder than their parents had done. They naturally wanted more from life but it would take a revolution of ideas to bring about this change. And the

change came, beginning with the Teddy Boys and the rock & roll scene of the late Fifties which gave young people a glimpse of what new life was possible. By 1965 the world of the young was altering dramatically, and the docile position occupied by previous generations was being landscaped with flowers and freedom. Come 1970 and youth had cut free from shackles and brought easier attitudes and fresh approaches to life. Life belonged to individuals; it was not a puppet for society to manage or a substance to be molded in a regimented fashion. Sixties youth demanded an unrestrained existence, and they got it, and for a decade or more the people of Britain lived in conditions verging on the sublime when compared with the dreary days of their elders. But the late Seventies met decline under the weak authority of a Callaghan Government and the country was bending at the knees and begging for radical changes that would enhance these new social conditions, not cause them to collapse amid scenes of industrial disaster. Thatcher arrived and brought with her the idea of individual prosperity for those who desired progress. The spirit of victory from the Falklands War 0f 1982 fuelled the feeling of well-being and a majority of British people grasped this golden opportunity to reach for their dreams. The once omnipotent God that had for centuries trespassed in the minds of the multitude was now being overthrown by the God of Money, for it was money that took the revolution of the Sixties to greater heights, money was the vehicle to success, and it was money that became the driving force of the bulk of society for the future.

169.　　　Vast areas of industrialized cities, especially those in the north, were filled by streets of back to back houses and through terrace houses built in late Victorian times. These streets formed friendly communities where neighbors knew neighbors well and where all children played together. But from the late Fifties, and all through the Wilson Governments of the Sixties and early Seventies concrete jungles of flats, maisonettes and other social housing began to replace them. Whole areas of terraces were demolished and caused communities to break up and disperse. Suburbs spread outward as cities changed in complexion and the modern three-bedroom semi became the aspiration of those who had once cherished the tiny back to backs. Ironically many Victorian streets outlived the concrete jungles which were poorly built; lots were demolished before the centuries turned. Today Victorian streets house many of today's city dwellers who are made up of students and immigrant populations, communities have adapted to a modern way of life and it is likely the back to back will survive well into the future.

170.　　　Although it is customary today for most people to own a bank account this was not the case in past decades. The method used by ordinary people to send money was by postal order purchased from a post office. Bank accounts were not necessary for workers were paid weekly in cash and few of them possessed excess money that could be placed in an account. To pay for goods or to send money by post an order to an equal value was bought. A standard charge was added to each order which carried a serial number and a perforated receipt to be retained by the sender. However, during the last quarter of the Twentieth Century, the trend towards monthly wages escalated and workers needed to have a bank account to receive their pay. Cheques replaced postal orders, and eventually, the plastic bank card superseded the cheque. Throughout this period cash transactions declined in all aspects of dealing with money. Perhaps as the Twenty-first Century unfolds cash will become obsolete.

171.   Seen daily on British streets the milkman was something of a national institution. He delivered milk to the doorsteps of the land and called for payment at the week's end. Few homes didn't have a milkman who was widely known in the local community. The national television advertisements that urged people to 'drink a pint of milk a day' supported this custom before milk was produced in plastic containers and sold cheaply in supermarkets. By the Eighties milk rounds were shrinking; profitability proved impossible and milk floats were quickly disappearing from streets. A few milkmen still ply their trade and attempt to keep it buoyant by selling dairy products, but in times of great competition the rounds are difficult to sustain and it seems their time is limited.

172.   The dolly tub and posser assisted housewives of the Fifties with their laundry. A dolly tub stood about thirty inches tall and was usually made of aluminum. It was filled with pans of hot water before the cleanest clothes were put in to wash. A wooden posser with three legs and a horizontal handle to rotate it to and fro was then immersed in the

water and twisted. This forerunner of the washing machine was strenuous to operate and tired a woman's arms. But after one set of clothes had been beaten by the legs of the posser the next set were put in, and this continued until the water became too soiled to clean any more clothes. By the Sixties washing machines were affordable and they came to relieve a housewife of one of her most exhausting tasks.

173.   The process of aging has undergone a remarkable revolution in the past sixty years. Both men and women of yesteryear appeared much older than their ages. Certainly, fashion had some bearing on their appearance but the skin too suffered from harder water, colder conditions, and few products aimed at body care. Today's sixty years old could well be mistaken for the over forties of earlier decades. Creams, soap products, healthier lifestyles, and comfortable living conditions have all slowed the aging process resulting in millions of elderly citizens with looks much younger than their forefathers.

174.   Cameras were the only affordable methods of keeping physical images of their children and loved ones for the working class of the post-war years. Cine cameras were not generally affordable so photographs became the sole cherished records of earlier life. But even photographs developed from a film were not cheap. When the photographer collected his photographs from the chemists or from the camera shop he had to pay for all of them: they may include out of focus snaps, snaps with cut off heads, or shots of the sky. It proved expensive and few people frequently took photographs due to developing costs. With

the advent of digital photography in the Twenty-first Century the camera became an everyday item of use; not only could poor images be swiftly erased but images could be edited and uploaded to a computer before printing. Photography today is not only affordable to the masses its quality of images is breath-taking to those who remember earlier cameras.

175.   The idea of a diet, or counting calories, would not have occurred to earlier generations: obtaining sufficient food for the needs of the family would have been a far greater priority. Food took a substantial proportion of income and it wasn't to be wasted or consumed wantonly. Few people of the Fifties and Sixties carried huge amounts of fat and the widespread availability of fast food was years in the future. Several social changes brought about the popularity of the diet, and the first is attributable to rising incomes and the relatively lowering in the cost of food items. Technology too played its part in the development of the couch potato as television and computers enticed people indoors and motor cars kept people off their legs: the daily pattern of exercise by walking consequently declined. And as the century reached its final decades and fast food, takeaways and ready meals gained appeal the usual practice of cooking home meals waned. Not only did people eat more, but they also ate unhealthily, and so put on weight due to lack of exercise. The dieticians' day had come and the era of the diet was here to stay.

176.   City bus queues resembled small crowds in the days before the motor car. It was not unusual to have to wait

until one or two buses were filled with passengers before an empty seat or standing place was free. The bus conductor placed his arm across the entry platform when the bus reached its maximum capacity, then he'd ring the bell, and away went the bus. For 90% of short-distance travelers, the bus was the primary choice. With so many routes threading across a city it was always possible to reach a destination without having far to walk. Through each decade from the Fifties bus travelers transferred to cars in vast numbers. Local councils attempted to halt the exodus with the sale of reduced cost passes for multiple journeys. They introduced park and ride schemes too, but largely their efforts proved futile for the independence afforded by the car could not be matched. By the first decade of the new century, the tide had turned completely and only 10% of people traveled on the bus. Bus lanes and articulated buses are among the latest ideas to address the decline in passengers but these too are likely to fail.

177.   The number of public libraries has fallen in recent decades and it seems destined to fall further. Librarians are attempting to stem the decline by opening cafes and introducing internet services: the task they face is unlikely to reap reward because the basis of library business is books. No amount of access to physical books can compete with the immediacy of a computer, and through advances in technology books from all ages can be acquired on devices specifically made for the reader. Although libraries of the past were incredible resources of education their place in the future is far from guaranteed.

178.   In the late Fifties and throughout the Sixties Ernie was spoken of with some affection. Ernie could make people's dreams come true and bring them riches. But ERNIE was merely a machine (an electronic random number indicating equipment) that was responsible for selecting winning premium bonds. The bonds were first introduced in Harold Macmillan's 1956 budget and very quickly became, with the football pools, the chief hope of working-class people to obtain instant riches. Premium bonds have survived through the generations and millions are still owned today: a top prize of £1million is on offer. The first ERNIE retired in 1972 and is currently on display at the Science Museum, London.

179.   There are grounds for believing that any statement about coffee drinking as a preference for tea drinking is subject to error. Coffee drinkers may predominate in some areas and through many generations in many ages, and the same may be said of tea drinkers but the evidence gained by the eye in the past sixty years seems to suggest that coffee drinking has steadily grown and tea drinking has declined somewhat. Today coffee appears to be the natural choice of younger generations who to some degree regard tea drinking as old-fashioned.

180.   A considerable change in attitudes to homosexuality has taken place in modern times. A practice, once thought grossly indecent by the vast majority of the public, and punishable by imprisonment, is now commonly talked about and proves no barrier to personal achievement or social standing. The Sexual Offences Act of 1967 stated that the

law would not prosecute consenting male adults who had reached the age of 21 for homosexual acts committed in private. The Criminal Justice and Public Order Act of 1994 reduced the age of consent to 18, and it was reduced further to 16 with the Sexual Offences Act of 2000. A similar Act of 2003 made it lawful for more than two men to commit homosexual acts. Much has changed in such a brief period of history both concerning homosexuals and in the number of openly homosexual men in society. Generally, these changes in law and perception do not affect those to who these changes do not relate, and only the future will determine whether such changes altered society in any significant fashion.

181.　　　The creatures killed on British roads are on the whole those which are endangered by traffic: whilst ever there are animals in the wild there will be victims. Over the past decades, populations of species have diminished, and therefore too the numbers of a defined species that are road-kill. Cats and dogs have always been victims of city traffic but as fewer dogs roam today they do not get killed so frequently. In the countryside of the past many species suffered; a journey along country roads may expose the body of one or more of the following: squirrel, stoat, weasel, shrew, rabbit, hare, and hedgehog. But man has committed the modern landscape to different purposes and the natural habitat of many creatures has reduced in size. No longer is this list of common victims relevant to some areas for the creatures are gone. Perhaps the most noticeable aspect of road-kill is the proportion of foxes killed in both rural and city areas. The fox never stood out as a victim in former times but due to its survival instincts and its adaptation to all environments, it roams wherever there is land to roam on. The bird will always be the most numerous of creatures killed by traffic, but of wholly wild landed animals the fox is presently a major victim of road deaths.

182.   Few obstacles disrupted traffic in the third quarter of the Twentieth Century: motorists paused at junctions, at a zebra crossing, and roundabouts. A journey by car used to be a trouble-free passage from departure to destination. Even city routes on main highways were uncluttered and several miles could be traversed without stopping. The final decades of the century brought about a change that modern drivers have come to accept but which has prevented a vehicle from traveling far without stopping. The traffic light, once placed at strategic points where main roads met, is now the curse of even short journeys. Stretches of the road less than two miles long may contain dozens of traffic light sets. Cities of the Fifties which may have displayed a hundred sets now possess thousands. A journey, even on deserted city roads at the dead of night, is interrupted as never before by a plethora of traffic lights.

183.   Income tax has undergone substantial changes since its highest rate peaked during World War II at 99.25%. Highest rates remained incredibly high until the Thatcher era of the Eighties, and it was due to this Prime Minister's belief in indirect taxation, that income tax rates fell nationally. Successive governments reduced tax on a working person's wage and over the past twenty-five years many poorly paid

workers have been taken from the lower taxation threshold altogether. However, income tax may have fallen consistently but the burdens on earnings are similar: with greater National Insurance contributions and an ever-rising Value Added Tax there appears to be little advantage gained by the average wage earner from this endless series of amendments to tax laws.

184.	The use of drugs is as ancient as the trade of prostitution, but public awareness and public use of drugs are much greater today than in any period in modern times. It was a rare topic of social concern in the Fifties, and even though drugs such as L.S.D. and marijuana are historically linked to the wild youth of the Sixties, it was never the real social issue that fictional writings and films seem to depict. The first 'drug' to be used by thousands of young people in Britain was glue, which gave rise to the cult of the glue-sniffer. Glue was affordable, and in the late Seventies and Eighties discarded glue bags could be seen on thousands of British streets and it was this explosion of drug-using youngsters that initiated the age of the drug culture. Throughout the coming decades as more cheap drugs became available their use permeated to other age groups. The numbers of heroin and cocaine users increased to worrying proportions: as the demand for drugs increased so too did the supply. The use of cannabis rose in direct contrast to the decline of the cigarette smoker and by the second decade of the current century cannabis was by far the most common drug on the streets of Britain. There are reasons to believe that society will have no option but to legalize the use of some presently popular drugs, for to criminalize the habits of such a huge proportion of society is not sustainable by law. Whilst ever vast numbers of otherwise law-abiding people engage in an act that is neither aggressive nor particularly harmful to other members of society is it unreasonable to punish them with a prosecution.

185.   The current worldwide community of poker players may be surprised how regularly an average 1950s adult in Britain played cards. Playing cards had a place in millions of households and proved a relaxing pastime for families across Britain. Games such as whist, solo, brag, rummy, Newmarket, and poker were fun for all generations. It was only with the increasing hours of television broadcasts that the playing of cards declined in popularity and by the end of the Sixties it was not usual to witness a family card-playing as it has been only a few years before.

186.   The early system of car number plates which used up to three letters and up to three numbers was exhausted by the early Sixties and replaced with the suffix of a single letter system that denoted the year of the car's initial registration. By 1982 the suffix system had reached the letter Y and a new system by which a letter preceded the number was in force. But vehicle growth soon exhausted this system too and in September 2001 a number plate contained 2 letters, 2 numbers, and 3 more letters.

187.   A majority of working-class women wore headscarves in the Fifties, and this trend continued for many years. The scarf was a method to protect a new hairstyle, or a recent visit to the hairdressers, from the elements. By

wrapping the head the hair retained its shape longer, and of course, provided warmth on cold days. However, both hairstyles and fashions changed and by the early Seventies, fewer women wore scarves. Although they can be seen today their use is chiefly continued by older women.

188.   By the late Fifties, more homes had a television than homes with a single radio. Television became the main source of family entertainment and was to remain so for the remainder of the century. But today's 24-hour programming schedule is relatively new. Programs were broadcast for a few hours in the evenings and television companies had sign-off periods during which screens were blank or a test card was viewed. In the Seventies and Eighties, program schedules were expanded until in 1987 Thames TV began broadcasting 24 hours a day; other companies followed, and with the advent of cable television in the current century which offered hundreds of channels the revolution of modern scheduling and viewer choice was complete.

189.   Stamp collecting used to be a hobby of many adults and schoolchildren in the days when letter writing was popular. In the post-war years, stamps from all over the world were easily obtainable by collectors and philately shops were far from rare on high streets. A new postage stamp was able to excite interest in a similar manner to a newly released pop song, but by the time the Seventies arrived fewer people, especially the young, were attracted to philately; other exuberant forms of entertainment made stamp collecting rather dull by comparison.

190.   Greengrocers and supermarkets of today would not get away with selling vegetables covered in soil, but in bygone years this was often the case. Clumps of earth were dried to the potatoes bought by housewives and even carrots could contain large amounts of soil around the bunch. The steady move to greater hygiene standards that became a feature of retail at the turn of the century witnessed the end of the vegetable in its harvested state. Presently all vegetables are sold washed, packed, and even dissected and the soil is no longer seen as a factor in preparing food for the table.

191.   A regular tradesman on the streets of 1950s and 1960s Britain was the chimney sweep with his bag of rods and brushes. With cities housing thousands of sooty chimneys his business was secure whilst ever coal remained a popular fuel. The chimney sweep extended his brush up the chimney by attaching rods and he covered the fire area with sheets to prevent soot falls to the hearth. Chimneys needed to be cleaned often to reduce the risk of fire. However, as gas and electric appliances replaced coal fires his trade diminished, and the few chimney sweeps that remain in business today deal more with chimney maintenance than the actual cleaning of soot from chimneys.

192.   During the past six decades, the English language has undergone something of a revolution, both nationally and internationally. The Queen's English, as correct pronunciation is customarily referred to, was spoken by a minority of British people during the first half of the Twentieth Century. Dialects proliferated, and they were both

regional and numerous. The language spoken in one area could be almost foreign in other parts of the country. Phrases such as 'put wood in t'hole' (close the door) littered the speech of most working people. In country places, dialects were more incomprehensible and country folks were often not understood by city dwellers. However, with the advent of television and with increased movement of people there came a general dilution of phrases – some became defunct and others blended into the language. The language itself was swelling at an enormous rate by the time the world and the media were internationalized. The places where dialects had existed for generations became infiltrated by outsiders and there was a gradual redundancy of words that had existed for centuries. Another consequence of internationalism was the need for a language used in diplomacy, a language with which to address a worldwide audience, and that language was English. As recently as the final quarter of the Twentieth Century is was unthinkable that a French President or a German Chancellor should publically speak English and it was usual for foreign news correspondents to be accompanied by interpreters for most parts of the world spoke in their own tongue. The English language expanded to encompass world culture and it became the first universal language of mankind. Today all people from all parts of the United Kingdom understand each other because they speak a common language which history has never before given them and it has drifted to distant parts of the globe where English is the second language of many millions of people.

193.   The garden has always been loved and cared for by the people of Britain, and for those lucky enough to own a garden in the post-war years they were an added means of survival because vegetables could be grown in the soil and cultivated in greenhouses. Often a rear garden was used for this purpose and a lawn and flower bed would be tended in the front garden. The garden was also a place for children to play and for a clothesline to be stretched between poles so the housewife may dry the washing. Pets, or sometimes chickens were kept there and usually, the man of the house had a busy time keeping up with outside duties. During the last quarter of the Twentieth Century, more people owned gardens, but their use changed in several ways. As people progressed with car ownership parts of the garden gave way to a driveway and in many cases a garage. Vegetables became cheaper to buy and new generations found it more convenient and less time-consuming to buy vegetables from supermarkets. Children too retreated from the garden into the house as computers stole their attention. And with the growth of garden centers and their various wares the nature of the garden underwent a decisive change: patios, conservatories, paving slabs, stones, gravels, plants never before available, decking, outside tables and chairs were purchased as garden improvements and they transformed these outside places into extensions of the living space. The garden which was once something of a necessity to upkeep became more the object of leisure time; a retreat where to relax with friends, or where time spent was a soothing change from the workplace.

194.   Of all social habits that of smoking has taken the greatest hammering in the past three or four decades. Once a habit of millions of men and women smoking took place in most locations. It is inconceivable to today's young generations that customers visited shops and smoked, visitors in hospital wards smoked around those ill in bed, and the uppers decks of buses were filled with dense clouds of cigarette smoke. Smokers were everywhere and few in society condemned the habit to a degree that it should be banned.   However, as medical evidence mounted that even passive smoking could harm health, and as hygiene became a greater issue in social thinking, the smoker became somewhat stigmatized and he was gradually encouraged to keep his habit to himself. By the first decade of the Twenty-first Century smoking in all public buildings was outlawed; the conscience of the smoker had been pricked repeatedly and thousands of smokers quit the habit. Today's high streets show few people openly smoking and few cigarette stubs litter the streets which are unlike the scenes of city streets of yesteryear.

195.   There has been a public shift in attitude to the police in modern times of which the cause is debatable. The role of the police in the third quarter of the Twentieth Century was perceived as that of public servants who worked for the amelioration of society. Policemen were individually known by communities for often they traveled on foot or bicycles and they had both the ear and the trust of common people. But gradually a vast majority of policemen were seen only in cars and at least in the public eye, they had separated

themselves from the communities they served. Their role as servants shifted by degrees to a role of controllers – modernization isolated them somewhat and the public trust began to dissipate. How significantly their actual practices have changed is also debatable, but today fewer members of society hold an attitude to the police that is similar to the one held by past generations.

196.   The professions of women have undergone radical changes throughout the last half of the Twentieth Century. In the Fifties and Sixties, a majority of employed females could be found in factories, mills, domestic service, nursing, the clothing industry, and shop work. Few women exceeded the expectations of their mothers but there were signs that improvement was on the way. More women were receiving higher education and the age of female liberation was about to explode. By the Seventies and Eighties, increasing numbers of females were being promoted to higher positions than before and the jobs which had hitherto been predominantly male environments were welcoming women. And when Margaret Thatcher attained the position of Prime Minister in 1979 the female worker had it confirmed that any achievement was possible. By the close of the century scarcely any position in society could not be occupied by a female and today women can be seen driving buses, working on motorways, sitting in Cabinet or being prominent scientists – the age of equality of the sexes has not only arrived, but it is also taken for granted.

197.   A peculiar habit of post-war people was to have a best room, usually the front room of their home which

remained deserted on weekdays. This room would be a special place for the family to assemble on Sundays, perhaps after a morning walk, then to repose in their best clothes, and behave in a rather sedentary manner. The best room syndrome does exist today in some households, but it is not tied so much to the Sabbath as in previous times.

198.   Canals which played a vital part in the Industrial Revolution serve a different purpose today than before the 1960s. Once they were major parts of the transport system and barges moved freight from its source to destination, but as road networks grew and faster means of transport became cheaper and cost-effective the canal systems declined rapidly. A new purpose was found for them by the leisure industry and individuals who liked life on the water. Many canals were restored during the last decades of the Twentieth Century as numbers of boat enthusiasts grew and spent increasing hours of leisure time on the waterways. Today many people live on marinas attached to canals and enjoy a different kind of life to that in the towns and cities.

199.   When the Poor Law was abolished by Attlee's post-war administration and replaced by the National Insurance Act 1946 and the National Assistance Act 1948 few could have predicted how the world would change over the coming sixty years. Welfare for all needy people, once a noble ideal was to be transformed into society's greatest burden on the public purse and those dependent on welfare were to suffer severe changes in public attitude towards them. In the beginning, a majority of claimants of benefits had no other choice but to seek assistance from a caring community: a

claim was more often than not a short term measure that helped individuals and families through hard times, as in the case of a man who had lost his employment and had no other form of income. But throughout the last half of the Twentieth Century, the number of people claiming welfare grew considerably until it became a widespread practice for both individuals and families to spend their entire lives existing on the contributions of taxpayers. Many thousands of others floated in and out of the benefits system which had long been overburdened and in need of reform. Of course, claimants who could once have felt relatively comfortable with their predicaments were now being classed as scroungers, idle, work-shy, and fraudsters: a proportion of the public had no sympathy for them because they were too numerous and too great a strain on society. However, it should be remembered that all governments from Attlee's to the present have been the architects of such a system and to blame people for a system that politicians created is ludicrous. For decades welfare in Britain has needed serious inspection and all governments have failed to act in radical enough ways to halt its collapse. It is easy to tell those on welfare to find a job or to work no matter how their incapacity or their disability affects them. But several factors occurring over the past decades make finding a job much harder than it used to be when labor was expensive. Huge numbers of immigrants now inhabit Britain, the great manufacturing industries of past generations have long been in decline and employ fewer workers, and the rules and regulations which restrict people's entrepreneurial spirit are abundant: it is useless to tell people to get a job if no jobs are to be found, especially by those who have few if any qualifications or specialist skills. For a country's welfare system to function as it is intended to relies on a vast majority of its citizens being taxpayers and with insufficient employment opportunities, this is presently unachievable in modern-day Britain.

200.   Media in 1950s Britain consisted of radio, emerging television, and newspapers. The public held no preoccupation with the media and many of life's pursuits were seen as more important. People gained the bulk of their knowledge through practical experience, books, and education; these were accepted forms of learning in a world that seemed still inaccessible and distant. Throughout the 1960s television expanded its reach and together with newspapers provided people with extra sources of information about what was happening in the world and although the news didn't come instantly it slowly began to arrive sooner than in the recent past because travel and communication improved. But as the Twentieth Century closed and both mobile phones and computers made their debut in society changes occurred that heightened interest in the media. It was aroused further with the advent of the world-wide-web which, it could be said that for many, life and the media blended as never before. New smartphones cemented the bond of young generations with the media. The internet in the first decade of the Twenty-first Century became the lifeblood of modern people and grew to be the primary source of both information and human

communication. The changes to social habits brought by television were staggering, but the new age of the internet advanced this change considerably. Media which had occupied a fraction of people's time in the Fifties became the foremost daily interest of the modern citizen.

Afterthoughts

The social revolution of the past sixty years has brought increased levels of comfort, intelligence, and liberty to the peoples of Britain. Those old enough to have lived through these decades perhaps reflect in dreams on the glories of yesteryear but the harsh realities of the past will hold little attraction for modern generations. Human progress in such a brief period has been astounding but the promise of what the Twenty-first Century offers is more astounding still.

In a century where millions of highly intelligent and exceedingly inventive people live and work there will be changes so startling that as yet they can't be envisaged. The enormous improvements in living conditions and society from 1950 to 2010 will be eclipsed by the staggering changes that will have occurred by 2100.

We can expect by the end of the century a Britain with a considerable population of robots and androids that may be indistinguishable from humans. The petrol and diesel engine cars will be obsolete, and the skyways rather than the highways will be bustling with traffic. Technology will harness power from the sun, the sea, the wind, and maybe from our bodies and almost every gadget that exists today will be a museum piece of tomorrow.

Politics of the future may involve a collection of professional country management boards and how Britain will fare with so many economically advancing nations as competitors for resources is not certain: perhaps our historical position as a major influence on world affairs will suffer.

By 2100 religion will scarcely exist, the population will surely be somewhat controlled, relationships may commonly endure for a brief period, and physical prowess will be greater than ever before. Morality will be different, animal populations will fall and the life expectancy of people will be beyond 100 years.

It is hard to guess what fashions will prevail or the type of synthetic food we may be consuming and even language, both spoken and written, will have undergone severe alterations. The monarchy is likely to end on our first experience of an incompetent monarch, crime and punishment will harbor new ideas developed by geneticists, and fresh diseases will arrive to replace those for which man has found cures.

A century is merely a fleeting spec of time in the life of the solar system, but for mankind living in Britain, the coming years will bring more innovation, more radical changes to our society than in all human history. We shall look back in 2100 and realize this upward curve of progress began its steep ascent from the 1950s onward.

THE END